THE
GREAT OUTDOORS
COOKBOOK

THE
GREAT OUTDOORS
COOKBOOK

Over 140 recipes for barbecues, campfires, picnics and more

PHIL VICKERY

Photography by Steve Lee

KYLE BOOKS

First published in Great Britain in 2011 by
Kyle Books
23 Howland Street
London W1T 4AY
general.enquiries@kylebooks.com
www.kylebooks.com

Printer line 10 9 8 7 6 5 4 3 2 1

ISBN 978-1-85626-919-3

Photographer: Steve Lee
Designer: Kate Barraclough
Home Economists: Clare Greenstreet and Wendy Lee
Prop Stylist: Jo Harris
Copy Editor: Jane Bamforth
Project Editor: Jenny Wheatley
Editorial Assistant: Estella Hung
Production: Nic Jones and Sheila Smith

A Cataloguing in Publication record for this title is
available from the British Library.

Colour reproduction by Alta Image
Printed in China by 1010 Printing International Ltd

CONTENTS

INTRODUCTION

Outdoor food has been a fascination of mine for many years. My father would often say to my mother, 'Doesn't food taste better outside', something that I did not really pay much attention to while I was growing up. The earliest memories of outdoor food I have are of coming home from school in the summer months to a house my parents bought in the late seventies. It had a large garden, with a vegetable patch and raspberry canes, and blackcurrant and loganberry bushes down one side. My mum would make us tea and we would have, wait for it, condensed milk spread on bread (my mother's favourite), banana sandwiches and also sugar sandwiches, sitting underneath the two cherry trees in the garden. By today's standards, not necessarily very good for you, but I distinctly remember the taste of them to this day – I'm sure because of the effect of the open air!

My dad used to take me out to gather flat mushrooms the size of a side plate, along with hazelnuts, chestnuts and the occasional walnut. Autumn Sunday nights were spent cracking open the hazelnuts and toasting the chestnuts. So when I became old enough to go fishing on my own with a good friend called Mark, it seemed to make perfect sense to catch a large perch, wrap it in foil and cook over a small fire next to the pond bank – again I can remember it really well, and the taste was superb. I progressed on to the occasional road-kill pheasant, wild ferreted rabbit, all cooked outside on an open fire; they seemed to taste completely different.

We camped as kids too and I loved it, and now I enjoy camping with my own children. I think the rise in what I call 'posh camping' – in shepherd's huts, old horse-drawn travelling caravans and bespoke large tents complete with wood-burning stoves – that you see advertised in the Sunday papers has also helped to popularise the great outdoors. Whether you're cooking on a barbecue, gas stove or an open fire, I hope you'll find inspiration in these pages to try something new next time you go camping.

Outdoor food in any shape or form is delicious; I have even written a whole section on the disposable barbecues you buy from a garage or home store. Yes, derided by many, but you can actually get brilliant results from a few simple ingredients. You'll also find flask food for winter and summer, snack food for people on the go, Dutch oven cooking, campfire cooking, and even a hog roast for the really adventurous!

American barbecue has become a real passion for me and I have spent many days researching, cooking and eating real barbecue food in the US. This culminated in making a film at Levi Goode's barbecue restaurant in Houston, Texas. There I had the best smoked brisket I have ever eaten in my life. Smoked overnight for up to 15 hours, it was superb. You'll see this influence coming through in several recipes in this book – I've included a mini smoking section in Chapter 8 as well as several slow-cooked barbecue dishes.

This book is a culmination of many years of outdoor cooking fun. I cook outside in all the seasons as you will see from the following chapters! I hope that you enjoy the recipes as much as I have cooking and writing them.

Chapter 1
BARBECUES AT HOME

It's a bit of a debate: gas or charcoal; and I get many letters from people asking me which they should cook on. Well, it's not a straightforward answer, as both have their merits and different cooking methods that they are suited to.

I tend to go for charcoal if I'm grilling, for instance burgers, steaks and chops. For what I call real barbecuing, by which I mean long, slow, indirect cooking, then gas is much easier to control and use. Having said that, many barbecue fanatics in the east coast of America would never dream of using gas – they prefer slow cooking with cool log smoke. But I think you can come pretty close to the real barbecue flavour using a gas grill, if you add wood chips or sawdust smoking boxes directly to the gas covers, to impart a pleasant smoky flavour.

In this section there are recipes for both areas of barbecuing. Some are really simple to make, while some are more elaborate in preparation and have very long cooking times, so check the recipe before you start cooking! Whether you are a seasoned barbecue cook, weekend fan or a total beginner, I hope there is something here for everybody.

Barbecues

To barbecue well, there are few simple guidelines that need to be followed. These will help you to make every barbecue a success. Below are tips for cooking on charcoal and gas, and some basic rules that apply to both methods.

CHARCOAL COOKING

* The first rule is to make sure that you have plenty of charcoal – there's nothing worse than running out!

* Always use an approved lighter fluid or gel, never petrol or diesel. If you use the latter, not only will your food taste of them, you probably won't get to eat it as you will be in hospital.

* Some people swear by lumpwood charcoal, but I prefer to use briquettes because they burn more evenly. For that reason they are also perfect for first-time barbecuers.

* Allow plenty of time for the coals to get hot. Start cooking when the coals are almost grey.

* Once you think you are ready, a simple test. Place your hand above the grill and count to 10. If you get to about 7 or 8 before pulling your hand away, it's the perfect heat for cooking. If you pull away at 3 to 4, then it will be too hot, and after 10 it's going to be too cool (although this is perfect for baking cakes in).

* Bank the charcoal on a gradient from one side to the other; this will give you a graduated cooking area. By that I mean a hot cooking area, mid-heat and a holding area for the food once it is cooked.

* A chimney starter is a great piece of kit for getting the coals going. Basically you fill the metal tube with charcoal, then light newpaper underneath. The coals then heat up very quickly and you can use the handle to carefully tip them into the barbecue.

* Apart from that, tongs, oven gloves and skewers are all you need.

* I sometimes like to add branches of bay leaves or rosemary to the barbecue when the embers are dying down. They impart a delicious herby flavour to the food – just take care not to let them burn, or they will add a slightly acrid flavour to the food.

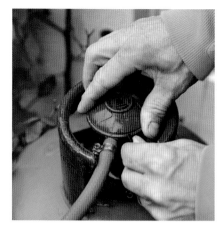  

GAS COOKING

* First and foremost, check all gas jets, pipes and connectors. Make sure regulators are free of any obstructions.

* Make sure the gas bottle is the correct one and you have plenty of gas.

* When lighting, make sure the lid of the barbecue is open, just in case it takes a few minutes to light and any gas can then disperse into the open air.

* Make sure you check regularly to make sure the barbecue has not gone out, even though this is a very rare occurrence (it's never happened to me but always best to be safe) and that the gas is still going into the barbecue.

* Finally have the barbecue serviced once every couple of years by a qualified dealer.

SAFETY

It goes without saying that you should be safe and aware when the barbecue is lit or on, especially when young children and adults who should know better (after a few too many) are in the vicinity. I have been to many barbecues where the man, generally drunk, putting on his apron with a print of a naked women's body in suspenders on the front says, 'right guys, let's get cooking' , and invariably ends up with a disaster on his hands – yes, you know who you are!

CLEANING

Never try and clean a barbecue when it is still hot. Leave it to cool and wait until next time you need to use it – just shut the lid and forget about it. When you are ready to use the barbecue again, heat it until really hot with the lid on and scrape off any charcoal cooked bits, mould and rubbish with a wire brush. Brush the bars with a piece of kitchen towel dipped in vegetable oil and you're ready to go.

This is a simple recipe, where half the marinade is used to add a tangy fruity flavour to the prawns, and the other half is served as a sauce.

Remember to oil the hot bars well to prevent the prawns from sticking!

Grilled Thai Prawns

SERVES 4 • PREPARATION TIME 10 MINUTES PLUS MARINATING • COOKING TIME 4–6 MINUTES

400g can pineapple in natural juice, *whizzed to a purée*

2 tbsp *nam pla* (Thai fish sauce)

juice and zest of 4 large limes

4 garlic cloves, *crushed*

1 tsp ground white pepper

1–2 pinches of salt

2 tbsp palm sugar

4 tbsp vegetable oil

2 pinches of chilli powder

20 raw freshwater prawns, *shelled but tails left on*

vegetable oil, for greasing

2 tbsp chopped fresh Thai sweet basil or regular basil

lime wedges, to serve

Place the pineapple purée, *nam pla*, lime juice and zest, crushed garlic, pepper, salt, palm sugar, vegetable oil and chilli powder into a medium bowl and mix really well.

Transfer half the marinade to a separate bowl and set aside in the fridge.

Add the prawns to the remaining marinade, mix thoroughly, cover and chill in the fridge for 2 hours.

Heat the barbecue to a high heat. Grease the bars well with a little oil dabbed on kitchen paper. Remove the prawns from the marinade, pat the excess off and place directly on to the bars. Cook for no more than 2–3 minutes on each side until well coloured.

Once the prawns are well coloured, remove and place into a deep serving bowl. Spoon over the chilled, reserved marinade, add the chopped basil, mix well and serve with the lime wedges.

I suppose the fact that you simmer the ribs in advance is cheating in a way. But I'm not too bothered by this as everyone is busy and if things can be made easier occasionally then that's fine by me!

For the very best results, start to prepare the ribs a couple of days in advance. That way you can leave the cooked ribs to marinate in the stock overnight and then leave them overnight for a second night for the rub to infuse its wonderful flavour.

Twice-cooked Beef Short Ribs

SERVES 4 • **PREPARATION TIME** 10 MINUTES PLUS CHILLING AND MARINATING • **COOKING TIME** 2¾ HOURS

4 short ribs, 1.3kg in weight

2 garlic cloves

2 onions, *chopped*

2 carrots, *chopped*

small sprig of fresh thyme

3 beef stock cubes

vegetable oil, for greasing

For the rub mixture

1½ tbsp English mustard powder

4 tbsp garlic powder or granules

1 tsp cracked black peppercorns

1 tsp dried thyme

For the mop sauce

1 tbsp clear honey

1 tbsp Worcestershire sauce

2 tbsp brown sauce

2 tbsp malt vinegar

1 heaped tbsp creamed horseradish

4 tbsp extra virgin olive oil

English mustard or hot creamed
    horseradish, to serve

Place the ribs, garlic, onions, carrots, thyme and stock cubes in a large pan. Cover with cold water and bring to the boil. Skim well and reduce the heat to a very gentle simmer. This is really important; if the meat cooks too quickly it becomes stringy, tough and dry. Cook, covered, very slowly for 2½ hours. Once cooked the meat will be very soft, but not falling off the bone.

Allow the ribs to cool in the stock and then transfer the pan to the fridge and leave overnight. Combine all the ingredients for the rub in a small bowl and mix well. Set aside overnight.

The next day remove the chilled fat from the stock and take out the ribs. Dry them well with kitchen paper. Sprinkle the rub all over the ribs, pressing down well. Cover and leave to marinate in the fridge for at least 1 hour or overnight.

Heat a gas barbecue to 225°C, or if you are cooking over charcoal the coals should be grey. When you are ready to cook, combine all the ingredients for the sauce in a jug.

Brush the bars with a little oil dabbed on kitchen paper. Carefully place the ribs on the hot bars and cook for 12–15 minutes, turning occasionally. You may have to place the lid on or down. Combine all the mop sauce ingredients and brush the ribs with it every few minutes – this gives the beef a beautiful flavour.

Remove the ribs from the barbecue and eat hot with a little English mustard or hot creamed horseradish.

No outdoor cookery book would be complete without a kebab recipe! My lamb version is packed full of flavour, and very easy to make. If you can make the mixture the day before it tastes even better.

I use twin skewers (see pages 218–219 for stockists) which are attached at one end, this ensures that the meat does not twist around on the skewer, so making it easier to cook on both sides. Alternatively moulding the meat into small patties also works well.

Moroccan Lamb Kebabs

SERVES 4 • **PREPARATION TIME** 15 MINUTES PLUS CHILLING • **COOKING TIME** 15 MINUTES

For the kebabs
500g ground lean lamb
2 tbsp chopped fresh coriander
2 garlic cloves, *crushed*
10 baby spring onions, *finely chopped*
3–4cm piece of fresh ginger, *peeled and finely chopped*
1 tsp ground cumin
1 tsp cracked black peppercorns
½ tsp dried chilli flakes
½ medium egg white, lightly beaten
2 tsp black onion seeds
2 tsp salt

For the coriander yogurt
200g thick natural yogurt
1 tsp finely chopped red chilli
4 tbsp chopped fresh coriander
2 tbsp clear honey
1 tsp ground cumin

To serve
4 large pitta breads
¼ iceberg lettuce, *chopped*
vegetable oil, for greasing

Place all the kebab ingredients in a large bowl and stir well to combine. Divide the mixture into four equal portions and mould each on to four flattened twin skewers. If not using skewers, divide the mixture into 8 equal-sized patties. Cover and chill well for at least 2 hours, or overnight if possible.

Preheat the barbecue, or if you are using a charcoal one then heat it until the coals are grey.

Combine all the ingredients for the coriander yogurt in a small bowl and set aside.

Lightly grease the barbecue bars with a little oil dabbed on a piece of kitchen paper. Brush the kebabs with a little oil – this will ensure the meat does not stick. Gently cook the kebabs on both sides for 4–5 minutes. Warm the pitta breads on the barbecue for 1–2 minutes, turning once.

Serve the kebabs in the pitta bread with the chopped lettuce, and a blob of the coriander yogurt. Serve the remaining yogurt on the side.

The best way to cook a large piece of lamb, such as the leg or shoulder is to 'butterfly' it. That's when it is completely boned, then cut open and laid flat – ask your butcher to do this for you. If you have a large kettle barbecue (a round one with a lid) or a gas barbecue, then you can cook this joint a lot quicker, as you can place a lid over the meat, then turn the heat right down and cook it evenly. If not, then you can cheat! Start the lamb in a preheated oven, at 180°C/gas mark 4, for about 45 minutes, then transfer to the barbie and finish off. This way you can completely control the cooking process, add the tasty barbecue flavour and get a nicely browned and glazed result.

Redcurrant, Mustard and Horseradish Butterflied Lamb

SERVES 6–8 • **PREPARATION TIME** 15 MINUTES PLUS MARINATING • **COOKING TIME** 1 HOUR 20 MINUTES–2 HOURS

5 tbsp creamed horseradish

2 tbsp wholegrain mustard

3 tbsp redcurrant jelly

2.5kg leg or shoulder of lamb, *boned, opened and laid flat*

4 garlic cloves, *cut into small, thin slivers*

4 tbsp olive oil

salt and freshly ground black pepper

redcurrant or mint jelly and new potatoes, to serve

In a small bowl mix together the horseradish, mustard and redcurrant jelly. Season well with a little salt and pepper and set aside. Make 15–20 small incisions in the lamb with a sharp knife. Insert the garlic into the incisions, pushing it well in. Spread the olive oil over the lamb, season well with black pepper and leave to marinate for 2 hours.

For the barbecue method Set up the barbecue for indirect cooking; if using gas, the temperature should be 180°C. Place the leg of lamb on the cool bars, place a tray or pan into the barbecue and fill with boiling water from a kettle. Cover with the lid, and cook the lamb slowly, for 1 hour, turning occasionally. Once the hour is up, spread over the horseradish mixture, turn up the heat, or move the hot coals over and cook the lamb until it is well glazed. This will take 2–3 minutes.

For the oven and barbecue method Preheat the oven to 180°C/gas mark 4. Place the lamb on a baking tray and cook it for 40 minutes. Preheat the barbecue; if using gas, set the temperature to 180°C. Spread the horseradish mixture over the meat. Carefully place the lamb on the hot bars and cook over a medium heat for 20 minutes until it is nicely glazed, turn over and continue to cook for a further 20 minutes. Take care not to burn the joint

For both methods Remove the lamb from the barbecue and leave it to rest, covered with foil, for 20 minutes. Slice and serve with more redcurrant or mint jelly and cooked new potatoes, at room temperature.

Baby Back Ribs with Spicy Ketchup Slather

MAKES 2 RACKS OF RIBS • PREPARATION TIME 40 MINUTES PLUS MARINATING • COOKING TIME 3½–4 HOURS

This recipe has three stages, but the end result is very good – so much better than any shop-bought ribs. Take your time, as this dish can take up to 4 hours to cook.

2 racks pork back ribs (15 bones each)

For the spice rub
2 tbsp paprika (I prefer smoked)
2 tsp freshly ground black pepper
4 tsp brown sugar
2 tsp salt
1 tsp celery salt
2 tsp chilli powder
3 tsp garlic powder
2 tsp English mustard powder
2 tsp ground cumin

For the basting sauce
100ml olive oil
250ml cider vinegar
200ml light beer, such as lager
100ml tomato ketchup
2 tbsp garlic powder
2 tbsp light brown sugar
1 tsp dried chilli flakes
1 tsp freshly ground black pepper

For the slather
8 tbsp tomato ketchup
2 tbsp vinegar (any type will do)
2 tbsp sugar
vegetable oil, for greasing

Combine all the spice rub ingredients together in an airtight lidded container. It will keep for up to 4 weeks. Mix all the basting sauce ingredients together in a jug and set aside for at least 30 minutes.

A couple of hours before cooking, remove the racks from the fridge. Turn them over: you will see a thin silvery membrane covering the inner bones. This has to be removed or the ribs will be as tough as old boots. Using a sharp knife, tease the fine membrane away from the tip of the rib; it will come away fairly easily. Then, using a kitchen paper to get a grip, pull away from the ribs and repeat the process with the other rack. Place the ribs on a baking tray, and sprinkle over half the rub, working it into the meat. Turn over and repeat the process until all the rub has been used up. Cover and place in the fridge for at least 1 hour, or overnight if possible.

Heat the barbecue to 150°C. Place a tray or pan on the barbecue and fill with boiling water from a kettle, place the ribs on the bars using the indirect method of cooking. Cover the barbecue and cook for 20 minutes. Brush over the basting sauce using a pastry brush or a new, medium-sized paintbrush, then repeat every 20 minutes, being quick so not too much heat escapes. Keep topping up the boiling water and keep an eye on the temperature – if the heat rises too much the ribs will end up dry and tough.

After 2½ hours, check the ribs – the meat at the ends of the ribs will have shrunk away, a clear indicator that the meat is probably cooked. Try and pull the ribs apart – if they do so with a little resistance, then they are cooked, if not then leave for a further 30–45 minutes. Remove them from the barbecue, along with the pan of water and turn the heat up to full.

Place all the slather ingredients in a small pan, mix together and bring to the boil. Brush each rack with the slather and lightly oil the bars with a little oil dabbed on a piece of kitchen paper. Place the ribs directly on to the hot bars and cook for a couple of minutes on each side to colour nicely, take care as they will burn very quickly. Serve with the rest of the slather sauce as a dip, beer, plenty of bibs and serviettes and tuck in…

These look great – they have a fabulous colour and taste delicious. Have patience though, they will take up to 4 hours to cook, but the longer and slower you cook the rolls the better the end result.

Most vacuum-packed meat is great for this dish as the moisture lets the marinade stick to the pork really well.

I like to serve the meat with Carolina Dipping Sauce and Slaw (see pages 187 and 194) or you could add a few Hush Puppies (page 211).

Paprika Pork Beer Belly Rolls

MAKES 2 ROLLS (8–10 PORTIONS) • PREPARATION TIME 5 MINUTES PLUS MARINATING • COOKING TIME 4 HOURS

2 x 1kg lean belly pork rolls, *boned, skinned and tied (ask your butcher to do this)*

For the rub
1 tbsp smoked sweet paprika
3 tsp soft light brown sugar
1 tsp chilli powder
1 tsp celery salt
1 tsp garlic salt
1 tsp English mustard powder
1 tsp freshly ground black pepper
½ tsp sea salt

For the beer wash
2 tbsp maple syrup
500ml bitter beer (I like Spitfire)
1 tbsp garlic powder
60g dark brown sugar
½ tsp red chilli flakes
1 tsp freshly ground black pepper

Place all the rub ingredients in a small bowl and mix well.

Place the pork belly rolls into an ovenproof tray and spoon the rub all over. Really work it well into the fat and meat. Cover and set aside to marinate for 1–2 hours at room temperature or better still, overnight in the fridge.

Preheat the barbecue to 160°C, and place the tray to the rear of the grill away from the front heat. Place a tray of boiling water on to the bars next to the meat, away from the direct heat if possible.

Close the lid and cook for 4 hours or until the internal temperature of the meat reaches 160°C (I use a meat cooking thermometer to check this). Combine all the ingredients for the beer wash. At 30 minute intervals, brush the joints with the beer wash quickly, and continue to do so every 30 minutes for the duration of the cooking. Be quick to keep the temperature constant.

Once cooked and well-coloured, remove the meat from the barbecue, cover with clingfilm and leave to rest for 30 minutes before eating – this ensures the meat will be tasty and succulent.

Cut into thick slices and serve with the Carolina Dipping Sauce, Slaw and Hush Puppies if liked.

This is a complex recipe but well worth the effort. For it to work really well, you will need a separate rotisserie attachment for the barbecue – the self-basting on the spit helps to give the duck a lovely, rich colour.

My Peking Duck

SERVES 4–6 • PREPARATION TIME 20 MINUTES PLUS MARINATING • COOKING TIME 2½ HOURS

2.5kg frozen Peking-style duck,
defrosted and giblets removed

For the marinade
6 tbsp dark soy sauce
2 tbsp sesame oil
1 tsp ground white pepper
2 tsp Chinese five spice powder

For the glaze
4 tbsp clear honey
1–2 pinches of salt
4 tbsp mirin
5 pinches of Chinese five spice powder
3 tbsp dark soy sauce
2 tbsp cornflour

For the dipping sauce
250ml plum wine
150ml mirin
100ml light soy sauce
2 tbsp black treacle
3–4cm piece of fresh ginger,
peeled and finely chopped
4 garlic cloves, *crushed*
4 spring onions, *finely sliced*
½ tsp dried chilli flakes
2 tbsp chopped fresh coriander

The day before you want to cook, place all the ingredients for the marinade in a small pan with 4 tablespoons water and bring it up to a gentle simmer.

Place the duck on a wire rack, and pop it into a deep tray – it should be nice and snug. Spoon the boiling marinade over the duck, covering all the flesh. Pour off the marinade, re-boil it and repeat the process a couple of times. This opens up the pores in the skin and takes in a little flavour.

Place the duck in the fridge, uncovered, and leave overnight – the longer the better, as this will dry the skin nicely.

The following day, preheat the barbecue to 180°C. Make the glaze by placing all the ingredients (except the cornflour) with 4 tablespoons water in a small pan and gently bringing to a simmer. Mix the cornflour with 4 tablespoons water and stir into the simmering sauce; it will thicken nicely. Remove and cool.

When ready to cook the duck, remove it from the fridge and thread it on to the rotisserie spit, securing well. Place on to the barbecue, with a small tray half filled with boiling water placed underneath, to catch the juices and fat. Start the rotisserie, cover with the barbecue lid and cook for 2 hours, basting occasionally with the glaze. Keep an eye on the temperature; if it browns too quickly, turn the heat down. While the duck is cooking, make the dipping sauce: combine the ingredients and leave for 1 hour.

Once the duck is cooked, paint on the glaze and increase the heat of the barbecue to 230°C. Cook for a further 20–30 minutes or until the duck is well glazed; you may want to brush it with some more glaze a couple of times. When it is beautifully golden, remove the spit from the barbecue and slide the duck off carefully. Cover with foil and leave to rest for 20 minutes. Carve and serve with the dipping sauce.

I don't normally agree with cooking oysters – I think they are perfect on their own. Having said that, sometimes I make an exception and this is one of those rare occasions. For this recipe I prefer to use Pacific oysters (native oysters are more expensive and frankly far too good). I serve them with mayo flavoured with wasabi – tangy Japanese horseradish.

Sometimes oyster shells can be an odd shape and may fall over on the barbie. If this looks like it is going to happen I get a baking tray, add small piles of salt or sand, and set the shells on the piles to steady them.

Warm Barbecued Oysters with Wasabi Mayo

SERVES 6 • PREPARATION TIME 20 MINUTES • COOKING TIME 3 MINUTES

6 tbsp good-quality mayonnaise

2 tsp wasabi paste

2 tsp soy sauce

18 fresh Pacific oysters, the bigger
  the better

finely grated zest and juice of
  2 large lemons

¼ tsp black peppercorns, *cracked*

Preheat the barbecue until it is fairly hot.

Place the mayo, wasabi and soy sauce in a small bowl and mix them together well.

Carefully open the oysters, using a proper oyster knife. To do this, take the oyster and place in into a clean tea towel, rounded shell down (an oyster has a flatter shell on one side). Holding the oyster with the cloth, place the knife into the hinge at the pointed end of the shell. There will be a slight lip. Move the knife from side to side while pushing it in slightly. You will find the knife will gently work its way into the shell. At this point, twist the handle of the knife and the shell should pop open. Lift up the shell, trying to keep as much juice in as possible and sever the muscle from the top shell. Remove any bits of shell.

Pour any juice into bowl through a sieve to get rid of any bits of shell. Remove the oyster from the bottom shell and place neatly back into the shell. Add a little of the strained juice.

When ready to cook, place the oysters, in their shells, directly on to the barbecue bars (or on a baking tray – see recipe introduction), making sure they sit nicely. Add a little lemon zest and juice and season. They will start to gently bubble and poach in the juice. At this point, carefully remove the oysters, add a small blob of wasabi mayo and eat straight away.

Naked, purely because they work perfectly well without any salt and pepper (nothing to do with what you're wearing!). But you can add as much or as little seasoning as you want or none at all.

For the perfect burger, I recommend beef with a 15–20 per cent fat content – chuck steak is ideal. I like to mince the meat on an 8mm plate and then a 5mm plate. Double mincing means the burgers will bind together easier and hold their fat and moisture better. Either mince the meat at home or ask your butcher to do it for you.

Naked Burgers

SERVES 6 • PREPARATION TIME 10 MINUTES • COOKING TIME 8–10 MINUTES

500g minced beef (15–20 per cent
   fat content)
3 tbsp dried natural breadcrumbs
vegetable oil, for greasing
salt and freshly ground black pepper
burger buns, to serve (optional)

Mix the beef and breadcrumbs together well, and add salt and pepper if you want to. Roll the mixture into 6 equal balls, and then flatten.

Heat the barbecue to a moderate heat.

Oil the burgers, very lightly, on both sides. Also, lightly oil the bars with a little oil dabbed on kitchen paper.

Grill the burgers for 2–3 minutes, then turn them through 90° (this gives an attractive criss-cross pattern) and continue to cook for a further couple of minutes. Flip the burgers over and cook the second side for the same amount of time and turning through 90° as before.

Serve the burgers on their own or in buns.

Leg or brown meat on turkey I believe makes better burgers, purely because the meat is juicier. I don't want to get too technical, but it's all to do with the leg muscles working harder and the meat from these areas having more flavour. Breast meat is fine also, but needs a little more attention when preparing and cooking. Skinned turkey breast can be less than 2 per cent fat, so when it cooks, it can cook slightly drier, leaving you with a crumbly texture. But I have discovered a great trick. If you add just a little mayonnaise to the raw mix it really helps to keep the burger beautifully juicy and tasty.

Juicy Turkey, Basil and Sweetcorn Burgers

SERVES 4–6 • PREPARATION TIME 20 MINUTES PLUS CHILLING TIME • COOKING TIME 10–12 MINUTES

500g minced turkey, (preferably
   leg meat)
2 tbsp mayonnaise
2 tbsp chopped fresh basil
2 tbsp Worcestershire Sauce
½ medium egg white, *lightly beaten*
2 heaped tbsp canned sweetcorn,
   well drained
4–5 tbsp dried natural breadcrumbs
olive oil, for spraying
salt and ground white pepper

For the mango yogurt mint dressing
200g plain yogurt
½ ripe mango, diced
handful of fresh mint leaves,
   chopped

To serve
4–6 flour tortillas
chopped iceberg lettuce
sliced ripe tomatoes

Place the turkey, mayonnaise, basil, Worcestershire Sauce and egg white in a bowl. Mix really well, then add the sweetcorn and breadcrumbs, season and mix well again. Leave the mixture to chill in the fridge for 30 minutes – the mixture will thicken up once the breadcrumbs reconstitute.

Roll the mixture into 4–6 equal balls, flatten slightly into small patties, then re-chill for 10–15 minutes.

Heat the barbecue to a moderate heat.

To cook, lightly spray the patties with a little olive oil (I use a plant mister filled with oil) then spray the bars quickly before you cook the burgers, this will stop them from sticking. Cook for 3–4 minutes then turn them through 90° (this gives an attractive criss-cross pattern), and cook again for 3–4 minutes.

Turn over and cook for a further 3–4 minutes and turning through 90° as before.

To make the dressing, mix the yogurt, mango and mint together in a small bowl.

Serve the burgers in flour tortillas with the iceberg lettuce, sliced tomatoes and a spoonful or two of mango yogurt mint dressing.

For this recipe to work, the fish has to be as fresh as possible and really well chilled. I add a little whisked egg white to the mixture, which helps to bind the fish together.

Salmon Burgers

MAKES 4 BURGERS • PREPARATION TIME 15 MINUTES PLUS 5–10 MINUTES CHILLING TIME • COOKING TIME 6–8 MINUTES

500g fresh salmon, free of skin or
   bone, as cold as possible
4 tbsp chopped fresh dill
1 tbsp grated fresh ginger
2 tsp Dijon mustard
2 tbsp mayonnaise
3–4 tbsp fresh breadcrumbs
1 medium egg white, *lightly whisked*
olive oil, for spraying
salt and freshly ground black pepper
Roasted Red Pepper Aïoli (see page
   194), to serve

Chop the salmon really finely, then re-chill in the fridge for 5–10 minutes.

Stir the dill, ginger, mustard and mayonnaise into the chilled salmon and season well with salt and pepper. Add a few breadcrumbs to the salmon mix, until firm, along with the egg white and mix really well.

Mould the mixture into 4 even patties, then re-chill in the fridge until you are ready to cook.

Heat the barbecue to a moderate heat.

To cook, lightly spray the patties with a little olive oil (I use a plant mister filled with oil) then spray the bars quickly before you cook the burgers – this will stop them from sticking. Cook for 3–4 minutes then turn them through 90° (this gives an attractive criss-cross pattern), cook again for 3–4 minutes.

Turn over and cook for a further 3–4 minutes and turning through 90° as before.

The flesh of the prawn or any shellfish for that matter makes a really fab burger. It is also a great base for adding flavours to. Here I add a little mayonnaise, to keep the mixture moist plus ginger, lime and a little kick of chilli.

The sherry dipping sauce has a nice powerful flavour balance and is the perfect accompaniment.

Prawn Burgers

SERVES 4 • PREPARATION TIME 20 MINUTES • COOKING TIME 6–8 MINUTES

2 tbsp olive oil

1 small onion, *roughly chopped*

2 garlic cloves, *finely chopped*

1 tbsp finely grated fresh ginger

500g raw freshwater prawns,
   shelled and de-veined

1 medium egg white, *lightly beaten*

2 tbsp mayonnaise

finely grated zest and juice of
   1 large lime

pinch of chilli power

olive oil, for greasing

salt and freshly ground black pepper

Dry Sherry Dipping Sauce (see
   page 191), to serve

Heat the olive oil in a small frying pan over a medium heat and add the onion, garlic and ginger. Cook for about 10 minutes to soften, then set aside to cool.

Really finely chop or better still, mince the prawn flesh (the finer the better) and then place in a bowl. Add the egg white, mayonnaise, lime zest and juice and season well with the chilli, a pinch of pepper and a couple of pinches of salt.

Shape the mixture into 8 small balls then flatten them slightly.

Oil the burgers, very lightly, on both sides. Also, lightly oil the bars with a little oil dabbed on kitchen paper, to stop them from sticking.

Heat the barbecue to a moderate heat.

Grill the burgers for 2–3 minutes, then turn them through 90° (this gives an attractive criss-cross pattern) and continue to cook for a further couple of minutes. Flip the burgers over and cook the second side for the same amount of time and turning through 90° as before.

Serve the burgers with the dipping sauce on the side.

Fresh tuna flesh makes a lovely burger and you can add a variety of flavours. Here I use a little softened red pepper, mustard and tarragon. I also add a little egg white to bind the mixture together, but this can be omitted if you want.

Tuna Burgers

SERVES 4 • PREPARATION TIME 15 MINUTES • COOKING TIME 4–6 MINUTES

2 tbsp olive oil

1 small red pepper, *very finely diced*

1 garlic clove, *finely chopped*

400g fresh tuna, *very finely chopped*

1 tsp Dijon mustard

2 tbsp chopped fresh tarragon

1 egg white

oil, for greasing

salt and freshly ground black pepper

Roasted Red Pepper Aïoli (see page 194), to serve

Heat the oil in a small frying pan, add the red pepper and garlic and cook to soften for 10 minutes. Leave to cool.

Place the tuna, mustard, tarragon and egg white into a bowl and mix really well. Add the cooled red pepper and garlic, and a little salt and pepper, and again mix well.

Mould into 4 small patties and chill well on a plate lined with clingfilm or greaseproof paper.

Heat the barbecue, and oil the bars well with a little oil dabbed on kitchen paper.

When ready to cook, lightly oil the patties with a little oil. Cook for 2–3 minutes on each side; leave the burgers slightly undercooked.

Serve with the Roasted Red Pepper Aïoli.

This isn't so much a recipe as a put-together job. It's best to use a rectangular block of ice cream so it fits into the sandwich, but any ice cream will do. I love the combination of hot and cold in this yummy pud!

Ice Cream Brioche Burger with Grilled Bananas and Crème Fraîche

SERVES 4 • PREPARATION TIME 10 MINUTES • COOKING TIME 10–15 MINUTES

250g rectangular block of vanilla
   ice cream
oil, for greasing
4 small bananas
500g brioche loaf, *cut into 8 equal slices*
4 tbsp good-quality strawberry jam
250g crème fraîche

Cut the ice cream into 4 small thick bars, if using the block version, and return to the freezer. If using regular ice cream you can just scoop it on later.

Heat the barbecue ready for grilling. Oil the bars well with a little oil dabbed on kitchen paper.

Place the unpeeled bananas on to a chopping board and using a sharp knife, slice just through the skin from top to tail horizontally on both sides. Brush the bananas with a little oil and grill for 4–5 minutes on each side. You will see they start to puff up slightly, exposing the flesh inside.

Grill the brioche slices for 1–2 minutes on the barbecue. Turn over and repeat, taking care as they will catch and possibly burn quite quickly. Keep them warm.

Open the bananas along the slits, and remove the top half of the skin.

When ready to serve, thinly spread the jam over the toasted brioche.

Place 4 brioche slices on to plates, and top with the blocks or a couple of scoops of ice cream, place the second slices on top. Blob on more crème fraîche and serve with the bananas alongside.

This is a nice simple pud – easy to make and it tastes wonderful. Once you've cooked your main course and the barbecue is starting to cool down then that's the time to pop the cake on!

Warm Golden Syrup Muffin Cake with Strawberries

SERVES 6–8 • PREPARATION TIME 15 MINUTES • COOKING TIME 20 MINUTES

500g strawberries, *washed, hulled and halved*

finely grated zest and juice of 2 large limes

2 tbsp icing sugar

vegetable oil, for greasing

350g self-raising flour

100g unsalted butter

120g caster sugar

120g golden syrup

250ml coconut milk

1 medium egg, *lightly beaten*

2 large ripe mangoes, *skinned and chopped into small pieces*

50g light brown sugar

sieved icing sugar, to dust

good-quality strawberry ice cream, to serve, optional

Mix the strawberries, lime zest and juice and 2 tablespoons of icing sugar together. Set aside until the cake is ready. Lightly oil two 22 x 15 x 3cm foil trays.

Place the flour and butter in a bowl and rub them together. Stir in the sugar, golden syrup, coconut milk and egg and mix well. Divide the mixture evenly between the prepared trays, then top with the chopped mango and brown sugar.

Bake the cake on the racks in the cooled barbecue for about 20 minutes or so, or until it is well risen.

Remove and allow to cool a little, then dust with the sieved icing sugar and serve with the marinated strawberries and a scoop of ice cream, if liked.

For this recipe, the barbecue has to be cooling off after cooking the main course. If you've used a charcoal barbecue, then the coals should all be grey and falling apart. On a gas appliance, use a low setting as the malt loaf browns really quickly indeed.

This is a different, but really yummy, way to finish off the perfect barbecue.

Griddled Malt Loaf with Peach Salsa

SERVES 6–8 • PREPARATION TIME 5 MINUTES PLUS 1 HOUR MARINATING • COOKING TIME 3 MINUTES

1 x 225g malt loaf, *cut into 6 slices*
25g unsalted butter
crème fraîche or vanilla ice cream,
    to serve

For the peach salsa
2 x 410g cans sliced peaches, *drained*
4 tbsp chopped fresh coriander
2 tbsp chopped fresh mint
¼ tsp dried chilli flakes
zest of 1 large lemon
4 tbsp lemon juice
2 tbsp dark brown sugar

Place all the ingredients for the salsa in a medium bowl, stir well and leave to marinate for 1 hour at room temperature.

Thinly butter the malt loaf slices on both sides.

Heat a gas barbecue to low or wait until a charcoal barbecue is starting to cool down. If the barbecue bars are too hot the malt loaf will burn very quickly indeed.

Place the bread on the hot bars and grill for 1–2 minutes on each side. Take care, or they will burn. The inside turns squidgy while the outside toasts perfectly.

Serve with the peach salsa piled on top and a large blob of crème fraîche or vanilla ice cream.

This recipe is perfect to cook once all the main course food is out of the way. I have found that once all the meat, fish or veg have been cooked if you place the lid back on the barbecue there will be enough residual heat left to cook this sponge perfectly.

You can cream the butter, sugar and eggs in advance, then when you are ready to cook all you have to do is to add the remaining sponge ingredients and layer it in the trays with the fruit.

Squidgy Tray-baked Summer Fruit Sponge

SERVES 4–6 • PREPARATION TIME 15 MINUTES • COOKING TIME 20–25 MINUTES

vegetable oil, for greasing
175g unsalted butter, *softened*
225g caster sugar
3 medium eggs, *beaten*
3 tsp baking powder
zest of 1 large lemon
2 tsp vanilla extract
250g fine polenta
500g frozen summer fruits
sieved icing sugar, to dust
raspberry ripple ice cream or thick
    cream, to serve

Lightly oil two 22 x 15 x 3cm foil trays.

Place the butter and sugar in a medium mixing bowl and cream them together. Add the eggs and mix thoroughly.

Stir in the baking powder, lemon zest, vanilla extract and polenta and mix well. Place one quarter of the mixture into each tray, then sprinkle one quarter of the frozen fruit over the sponge in each tray.

Divide the remaining sponge evenly between the trays and finally divide the fruit between the trays.

Bake the cake in the cooled barbecue for 20–25 minutes or until well-risen.

Once cooked, remove carefully, and leave to rest for 10 minutes, then dust well with icing sugar and serve with raspberry ripple ice cream or thick cream.

Chapter 2
BARBECUES ON THE GO

Over the past few years disposable bar barbecues have become very popular. There is not a petrol station, DIY store, supermarket or corner shop that does not stock them over the summer months. They come in various sizes, and are a really great piece of kit for the outdoor cook – easy to buy, use and work with. I love them, my only problem is with people who leave them lying around once they have finished with them.

I think the main point to mention here as with almost all outdoor cooked food is preparation. If you spend a couple of moments getting ready such as trimming meat, making sauces, getting the basic ingredients prepared and ready to go, then the day will be much more enjoyable and less fraught. The last thing you want is to be under pressure once you light the barbecue.

A couple of helpful tips are to lightly oil the food and the hot bars with a little oil. This will prevent the food from sticking, especially when the food to be cooked is slightly wet from a marinade or dressing. And always light the barbecue and leave it until you have three or four black tips left on the charcoal, this really is a good indicator of a perfect heat to cook on.

I use a disposable barbecue bag to cook several recipes in this chapter. This is a brilliant way to cook fish as it part-steams in the parcel with the flavours of all the herbs or spices you add. If you can't get hold of the bags, use a well-sealed double layer of foil instead.

This may sound like an odd combination but it actually works very well indeed! Simply bake the potatoes in the oven before you head out, pop the other bits and pieces in a freezer bag and you're ready to go.

Twice Cooked Sweet Potatoes with Taramasalata and Smoked Paprika

SERVES 4 • PREPARATION TIME 10 MINUTES PLUS CHILLING TIME • COOKING TIME 1 HOUR

4 medium-sized sweet potatoes,
  scrubbed
vegetable oil, for greasing
2 tbsp olive oil
¼–½ tsp smoked paprika
200g taramasalata
4 tbsp chopped fresh basil
1 large lime, *halved*
salt and freshly ground black pepper

Preheat the oven to 200°C/gas mark 6. Prick the sweet potatoes all over with a fork and place on a baking tray. Bake for about 40–45 minutes, or until cooked through (alternatively you could microwave the potatoes for about 10–15 minutes or until cooked through). Set the cooked potatoes aside to cool, cut them in half lengthways and place in an airtight lidded container. Chill the potatoes in the fridge until you are ready to get going.

Light a disposable barbecue and when a few tips of the charcoal are still black, but the rest are grey, it is ready to cook on. Lightly oil the bars with a little oil dabbed on kitchen paper, this will stop the potatoes from sticking.

Drizzle the cut sides of the potatoes with half the olive oil and then season with salt, pepper and paprika, rubbing it in well. Cook the potatoes, seasoned side down, for 6–7 minutes. Oil the backs of the potatoes and season again, then flip over and cook for a further 5–6 minutes.

Once warmed through, transfer to a serving plate. Top each potato half with taramasalata and sprinkle over a little paprika and chopped basil. Squeeze over the lime juice and serve.

*Cooking outdoors must be simple; here is another great example of that –
really tasty, fresh food that is straight to the point.*

Grilled Fresh Asparagus with Lemon Olive Oil and Sweet Mustard Mayo

SERVES 4 • PREPARATION TIME 10 MINUTES • COOKING TIME 10–12 MINUTES

For the mayonnaise

6 tbsp mayonnaise

1 tsp sugar

3 tbsp wholegrain mustard

4 tbsp roughly chopped fresh parsley

For the asparagus

500g fresh young asparagus

2 tbsp olive oil

vegetable oil, for greasing

1 large lemon, *halved*

salt and freshly ground black pepper

Make up the mayonnaise before you leave home by mixing all the ingredients together well. Spoon into a screw-top jar or lidded container and chill until ready to use.

Place the asparagus in a lidded airtight container and spoon over the olive oil. Season and toss to coat.

Light a disposable barbecue and when a few tips of the charcoal are still black, but the rest are grey, it is ready to cook on.

Lightly oil the bars with a little oil dabbed on kitchen paper, this will prevent the asparagus from sticking.

Place the asparagus on the barbecue and grill for 5–6 minutes, then carefully turn over and cook for a further 5–6 minutes.

Squeeze over the lemon juice and serve straight away with the sweet mustard mayo for dipping.

Grilled Chicken Wings
with Spicy Peanut Dressing

SERVES 4 • PREPARATION TIME 15 MINUTES PLUS CHILLING AND MARINATING TIME • COOKING TIME 50 MINUTES

A great way to cook chicken wings for the barbecue is to poach them gently first. Then all you need to do is to finish them off on the barbecue.

The spicy peanut sauce is delicious with the chicken. Make it up at home and take it with you.

16 chicken wings

1 carrot

1 onion, *chopped*

1 chicken stock cube

1 tbsp toasted sesame oil

2 tbsp Worcestershire Sauce

pinch of chilli powder

pinch of ground cumin

vegetable oil, for greasing

salt and freshly ground black pepper

For the sauce

2 tbsp vegetable oil

1 small onion, *chopped*

2 garlic cloves, *finely chopped*

340g jar crunchy peanut butter

1 tbsp maple syrup

couple of dashes of Tabasco Sauce

4 tbsp chopped fresh coriander

pinch or two of chilli powder

2 tbsp malt vinegar

Remove the tips from the wings and discard, then cut each wing in half through the bone. Place the chicken wings in a pan, add the vegetables and stock cube, cover with cold water. Bring to the boil, turn down the heat, so the chicken is just simmering. Season well and cook gently for 15 minutes. The meat should be cooked, but not falling off the bone.

When the chicken wings are cooked thoroughly, strain them and set aside to cool. Transfer them to an airtight lidded container and chill in the fridge.

Once the wings are chilled, add the sesame oil, Worcestershire Sauce, chilli powder and ground cumin to the container, and mix well to coat the chicken. Set aside in the fridge to marinate until you are ready to cook.

To make the sauce, heat the vegetable oil in a saucepan, and add the onions and garlic. Cook for 15 minutes to soften.

Add the remaining ingredients and enough cold water to make a yogurt consistency. Just warm it through gently – do not let it boil. Adjust the seasoning, then transfer to an airtight lidded container and leave to cool. Chill until needed.

Light a disposable barbecue and when a few tips of the charcoal are still black, but the rest are grey, it is ready to cook on. Lightly oil the bars with a little oil dabbed on kitchen paper.

Grill the chicken wings for 3–4 minutes on each side until well browned.

Serve hot with the chilled peanut sauce separately (you may need to add a little water to the sauce to thin it out after it has been chilled).

Grilled Black Pepper Rib Eye Steak Wraps with Creamed Horseradish, Rocket and Red Peppers

SERVES 4 • **PREPARATION TIME** 15 MINUTES • **COOKING TIME** 10–15 MINUTES

Rib eye is my favourite cut of steak – it is full of flavour due to the fat content. Just prepare the peppers and the steak before you go and once you light the barbecue the rest is easy.

Once you have put the wraps together, you can pop them on the barbecue to toast the tortillas a little, or to keep them warm.

4 tbsp olive oil

2 red peppers, *deseeded and cut into thin strips*

2 x 225g rib eye steaks

oil, for greasing

4 large flour tortillas

50g rocket

2 tbsp creamed horseradish

salt and freshly ground black pepper

Heat half the olive oil in a frying pan and add the peppers with a little salt and pepper. Cook for 5–8 minutes or until soft and lightly coloured. Leave to cool, then transfer to an airtight lidded container and chill.

Cut each steak into 8 thin strips and place in a plastic bag. Add the remaining olive oil and a little black pepper, close the bag and shake well. Chill well until you want to cook.

Light a disposable barbecue and when a few tips of the charcoal are still black, but the rest are grey, it is ready to cook on.

Lightly oil the bars with a little oil dabbed on kitchen paper, this will prevent the steak from sticking. Place the steak strips onto the hot bars and cook for 2–3 minutes on each side.

Meanwhile, lay the tortillas out, sprinkle the cooked pepper and rocket evenly on top and spoon on a little horseradish.

Once the steak is cooked, add to the tortillas and roll up. Cut in half and eat – easy and delicious.

This is probably one of the most popular barbecue dishes that I make. Prepare the sauce and chicken before you leave home, then all you have to do is to pop the chicken on the barbie and relax.

The sauce will thicken slightly when it is cool, so add a little more water for a silkier sauce if you like.

Grilled Chicken and Air Dried Ham Skewers with Spicy Peanut Dipping Sauce

SERVES 4 • PREPARATION TIME 15 MINUTES • COOKING TIME 15–20 MINUTES

For the sauce

120g crunchy peanut butter

pinch of chilli powder

juice of 2 lemons

2 tbsp finely chopped coriander, optional

For the skewers

2 skinned chicken breasts, *each cut into 6 thin strips*

6 slices air-dried ham, *each cut into 2 lengthways*

vegetable oil, for greasing

salt and freshly ground black pepper

8 wooden skewers

Soak the skewers in cold water. To make the sauce, place the peanut butter, chilli powder, 8–10 tablespoons water and the lemon juice in a small pan and gently heat until you have a sauce consistency. Add the coriander, transfer to an airtight lidded container and chill until needed.

Thread the chicken on the skewers, then wrap the ham strips around the chicken. Secure either end of the ham on the skewer.

Light a disposable barbecue and when a few tips of the charcoal are still black, but the rest are grey, it is ready to cook on.

Lightly oil the chicken and the barbecue with a little oil dabbed on kitchen paper. Season the kebabs and cook for 8–10 minutes on each side, until cooked through.

Serve hot, with the chilled peanut sauce separately (you may need to add a little water to the sauce to thin it out after it has been chilled).

This is a lovely way of getting not only more succulence into a chop but also more flavour. Twenty minutes of brining will make a world of difference to the texture and taste of the chop!

You may find that the brined meat will brown slightly quicker than usual, so keep a close eye on the chops once you start cooking.

4 x 2cm thick, boned, skinned
   pork chops or boneless cutlets
2 tbsp olive oil
oil, for greasing

For the brine
30g granulated sugar
15g salt

For the salad
2 heads of chicory
juice of 1 small lemon
6 tbsp mayonnaise
4 cooked crispy streaky bacon
   rashers, *finely chopped*
freshly ground black pepper

Simple Brined Chops with Bacon and Chicory Salad

SERVES 4 • **PREPARATION TIME** 20 MINUTES PLUS MARINATING • **COOKING TIME** 15–20 MINUTES

To make the brine, place the sugar, salt and 300ml water in a pan. Bring to the boil to dissolve the sugar and salt. Set aside to cool.

Press the pork chops out with the back of a knife to stretch them slightly and then place in a glass, ceramic or stainless steel bowl.

Check the total weight of the brine, it should weigh 345g. If it is less than this, make up the difference with cold water.

Pour the cold brine over the chops and mix well, then leave to marinate for 20–30 minutes. After this time, remove the chops and pat them dry. Chill until needed.

Meanwhile, make the salad. Slice the chicory very finely, then add the lemon juice and mix well, this will prevent the chicory discolouring too much. Stir in the mayonnaise and crispy bacon and season well with black pepper. Mix really well, transfer to an airtight lidded container and chill until needed.

Light a disposable barbecue and when a few tips of the charcoal are still black, but the rest are grey, it is ready to cook on.

Lightly oil the chops on both sides with the olive oil and season them with black pepper. Oil the barbecue with a little oil dabbed on kitchen paper. Cook the chops for 7–8 minutes on each side or until cooked through.

Serve the chops with the bacon and chicory salad.

This is a nice twist on old favourite which is traditionally cooked in a tandoor – a large, very hot, clay oven. I use a barbecue bag (see Resources, page 218), which part-steams the fish with all the lovely fragrant spices and my number one herb – coriander. If you can't get hold of them, use a well-sealed double layer of foil instead.

Chop-cut Tandoori-Style Bass

SERVES 2 • PREPARATION TIME 15 MINUTES PLUS 5 MINUTES COOLING • COOKING TIME 10–20 MINUTES

1 x 500–750g bass, *gutted, scaled and head removed*

1 tbsp vegetable oil

finely grated zest and juice of 1 small lemon

½ tsp dried chilli flakes

2 garlic cloves, *finely chopped*

½ tsp ground cumin

½ tsp ground coriander

½ tsp garam masala

½ tsp ground turmeric

1 tbsp tomato purée

200g natural yogurt

small bunch of fresh coriander, *roughly chopped*

salt and freshly ground black pepper

disposable barbecue bag or aluminium foil

Cut the bass into 2 or 3 pieces widthways.

Mix all the ingredients apart from the yogurt and coriander in a bowl and season well with salt and pepper. Stir in half the yogurt and half the chopped coriander. Add the bass and rub the paste all over it. Cover and set aside in the fridge until ready to cook.

Mix the remaining yogurt and coriander together. Transfer to a lidded airtight container and chill.

Place the marinated fish in the disposable barbecue bag and seal well.

Light a disposable barbecue and when a few tips of the charcoal are still black, but the rest are grey, it is ready to cook on.

Place the bag on the barbecue and cook for 10–20 minutes. Once cooked, remove and set aside for 5 minutes to cool.

Open the bag and serve the fish with the coriander yogurt.

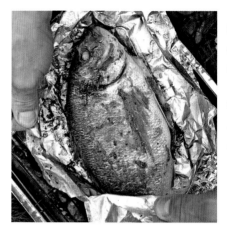

Cooking a whole fish in a barbecue bag is a simple way to make sure it doesn't stick to the grill – and you don't lose any of the cooking juices either. Any whole fish, weighing around 400g, will work.

Prepare everything the day before, then you can just pack the bags of fish and fennel in a freezer bag and head out. Cooking times will vary though, so keep an eye on the fish.

Whole Bream with Red Pesto and Shaved Lemon Fennel

SERVES 2 • PREPARATION TIME 20 MINUTES • COOKING TIME 12–15 MINUTES

1 large fennel bulb

2 tbsp extra virgin olive oil

finely grated zest and juice of
    2 large lemons

1 whole bream, about 400g, *scaled,
    gutted and head removed*

2 tbsp red pesto

50g basil leaves

salt and freshly ground black pepper

disposable barbecue bag or
    aluminium foil

.

Finely shave the fennel, I like to use a Japanese mandolin to do this (available from most good catering outlets or online). Place the fennel in a bowl and add the oil, lemon zest and juice with a little salt and pepper and mix really well. Pop into a sealable plastic bag and chill well.

Wash the bream well, then dry it inside and outside with kitchen paper. Spoon the pesto into the cavity of the bream, and smear any left on the outside of the fish. Place into a disposable barbecue cooking bag, add a dash of water and seal well. This can all be done a day in advance.

Light a disposable barbecue and when a few tips of the charcoal are still black, but the rest are grey, it is ready to cook on.

Place the bag with the fish in on to the hot barbecue for 12–15 minutes. Open the bag of fennel (it will smell amazing!), and tip into a bowl. Add the basil and mix well.

Once the fish is cooked, open the bag and eat it straight away with the fennel.

I really love this idea – you make the base at home and then leave the chicken to marinate. When you're ready to cook, just transfer it into a barbecue bag and take it with you – an alternative takeaway! Once cooked, there's no washing up, apart from cutlery – a really tasty, savoury summer treat.

I like to serve this with warmed chapatti – simply heat them through on the barbie for a few minutes.

Real Easy Chicken Korma

SERVES 2 • **PREPARATION TIME** 15 MINUTES PLUS 5 MINUTES RESTING • **COOKING TIME** 15–20 MINUTES

2 tbsp vegetable oil

¼ tsp dried chilli flakes

½ tsp ground turmeric

½ tsp ground cumin

¼ tsp garam masala

½ onion, *finely chopped*

2 tsp finely chopped fresh ginger

2 garlic cloves, *chopped*

100ml lager

½ chicken stock cube

2 tbsp double cream

½ tsp sugar

2 small chicken breasts, *skinned and cut into 1cm pieces*

1 tsp cornflour

2 chapattis, *to serve*

disposable barbecue bag or aluminium foil

Heat the oil in a small frying pan, add the spices and toast them slightly, being careful not to let them burn. Add the onion, ginger and garlic and sauté for a couple of minutes. Add the lager and stock cube and cook until the liquid is reduced by half. Pour in the cream and mix well, add a little sugar to taste, and then set aside to cool.

Coat the chicken in the cornflour, then add to the cooled sauce and mix well. Chill until ready.

Pour or spoon the chicken and sauce into a disposable barbecue cooking bag and seal well. This can be prepared up to a day in advance.

Light a disposable barbecue and when a few tips of the charcoal are still black, but the rest are grey, it is ready to cook on. Place the bag on the barbecue and cook for 15–20 minutes or until ready – the chicken will have turned opaque. Once cooked, remove the bag from the barbecue and place it on a plate, then set aside to rest for 5 minutes.

Meanwhile place the chapattis on the barbecue and warm them through on both sides for 1–2 minutes while the chicken is resting.

When ready, open the cooking bag carefully, and serve the curry with the warmed chapatti.

This fresh, delicate marinade works well with either fish or meat cooked on a barbecue but I particularly like it with prawns. The secret is to not cook the marinade for too long, then it will keep its lovely, fresh flavours.

Five Spice Marinated Prawns

SERVES 2 • PREPARATION TIME 15 MINUTES PLUS 10 MINUTES RESTING • COOKING TIME 10–15 MINUTES

2 spring onions, *finely sliced on the diagonal*
8 large raw freshwater prawns, *shelled but tails left on*
salt and freshly ground black pepper

For the marinade
200ml mirin
100ml soy sauce
2 tsp Chinese five spice powder
2 tbsp very finely chopped fresh ginger
3 garlic cloves, *finely chopped*
1 tbsp toasted sesame oil
finely grated zest and juice of 2 large limes
½ tsp finely chopped red chilli

disposable barbecue bag or aluminium foil

Place all the marinade ingredients in a small pan and bring just to the boil. Remove from the heat and set aside to cool.

Add the spring onions to the pan and check the seasoning. Add the prawns and set aside until ready to cook.

Place the prawns and marinade in a disposable barbecue cooking bag just before cooking.

Light a disposable barbecue and when a few tips of the charcoal are still black, but the rest are grey, it is ready to cook on.

Place the bag on the barbecue and cook for 10–15 minutes, or until the flesh is opaque. Remove from the barbecue and leave to rest for 10 minutes.

Open the bag and tuck in.

I love mussels, however they are cooked! This is a quick way to enjoy them – straight from the bag.

Marsh samphire, sometimes known as 'sea asparagus' is a plant that grows wild on the coast. You can often pick it up at fishmongers and farmers' markets. If you can't get hold of it, just omit it from the recipe.

Steamed Mussels with Chilli, Lime, Garlic and Coriander

SERVES 2 • PREPARATION TIME 25 MINUTES PLUS 5 MINUTES RESTING • COOKING TIME 10–20 MINUTES

2 tbsp vegetable oil

½ small onion, *roughly chopped*

2 cloves garlic, *chopped*

2 stalks lemongrass, *bruised*

20g fresh ginger, *peeled and sliced into fine strips*

pinch of dried chilli flakes

200ml coconut milk

½ fish stock cube, *crumbled*

3 tsp Thai green curry paste

500g fresh mussels, *cleaned*

1 small bunch fresh coriander, *roughly chopped*

1 small bunch samphire (about 100g)

disposable barbecue bag or aluminium foil

Heat the oil in a medium pan, then add the onion, garlic, lemongrass, ginger and chilli flakes and cook for 5 minutes to soften slightly.

Add the coconut milk, stock cube and curry paste and simmer very gently for 15 minutes. Set aside to cool.

Once the sauce has cooled, place the mussels in a disposable barbecue cooking bag. Pour over the cold sauce, add the coriander and samphire, mix thoroughly, then seal well.

Light a disposable barbecue and when a few tips of the charcoal are still black, but the rest are grey, it is ready to cook on.

Place the bag on the barbecue and cook for 10–20 minutes, or until all the mussels have opened.

Remove carefully from the barbecue and set aside to rest for 5 minutes.

Open the bag and eat with a spoon and fork.

For this to work the mango has to be really ripe, as all you are doing is warming through the soft, sweet flesh.

Make sure you hull the strawberries after you wash them, otherwise they will fill with water and go soggy!

Grilled Chilli Mango with Sweet and Sour Strawberries

SERVES 4 • PREPARATION TIME 15 MINUTES • COOKING TIME 4–6 MINUTES

2 medium-sized ripe mangoes

2 tbsp oil

½ tsp dried red chilli flakes

1 tbsp caster sugar

1 tbsp white wine or cider vinegar

150g strawberries, *washed, then hulled and halved, in that order*

vegetable oil, for greasing

crème fraîche, to serve, optional

Cut the sides off each mango (leaving the skin on), by cutting lengthways with a knife. Keep the knife parallel to the side of the stone as you cut. Pat the cut sides really dry with kitchen paper, then lightly oil with 1 tablespoon of the oil and dust over a few chilli flakes.

When you are ready to cook, sprinkle the sugar and vinegar over the strawberries and gently stir. Leave the strawberries to marinate while you are cooking the mangoes and they will make their own syrup.

Light a disposable barbecue and when a few tips of the charcoal are still black, but the rest are grey, it is ready to cook on.

Lightly oil the heated barbecue grid with a little oil dabbed on kitchen paper.

Place the cut side of the mangoes on to the hot bars and cook for 1–2 minutes. Oil the skin side of the mango with the remaining 1 tablespoon of oil and turn over, then cook for a further 3–4 minutes.

Serve the cooked mangoes with a spoonful of marinated strawberries and a blob of crème fraîche.

Chapter 3
FEAST ON 1 OR 2 RINGS

I cook on simple gas burners regularly – they are really easy to use because they provide instant heat – it's basically like moving your stove outside. They are also relatively cheap and widely available and are perfect for camping and caravanning.

The secret here is to prepare everything before you set out, if you can. This, I agree, is sometimes easier said than done, especially if you have just turned up at a campsite, or have travelled miles and had to buy the ingredients en route or at the site you are stopping at. But a little forward planning will make a massive difference when you eventually start to cook.

I have tried to keep the ingredients and utensils to a minimum in this chapter for obvious reasons, and suggest that you only really need two or three pans with lids to cook all the dishes. I have also tried to make the recipes as simple as I can, while making sure they are well-balanced, nutritious and of course packed full of flavour.

This simple one-pot dish cooks very quickly so is ideal for cooking on a camping stove or in a caravan. It is packed full of vegetables and is a great filling vegetarian meal.

When I go camping I like to pack small sachets of mayonnaise in my essentials box – they are lighter to carry than a bottle of oil, and work well for sautéing vegetables and meats. Basmati rice probably has the best flavour, but long grain will be fine too.

Courgette, Pea and Parmesan Pilaff

SERVES 2 • PREPARATION TIME 10 MINUTES • COOKING TIME 15 MINUTES

4 small sachets of mayonnaise
   or 4 tbsp oil
1 medium onion, *chopped*
1 tsp turmeric
2 tsp cumin seeds
2 mugfuls of basmati or long
   grain rice
small glass of white wine, optional
1 vegetarian stock cube
1 small courgette, *cut into 1cm cubes*
220g can chickpeas, *drained*
handful of frozen peas, *defrosted*
4 tbsp chopped fresh coriander,
   optional
handful of grated Parmesan cheese
salt and freshly ground black pepper

Heat the mayonnaise or oil in a medium saucepan, with a tightly-fitting lid. Add the onion, turmeric and cumin seeds and cook for 3–4 minutes until the onion has softened.

Add the rice, wine (if using), crumbled stock cube, 4 mugfuls of water, the courgette, chickpeas, frozen peas and coriander. Season well with salt and pepper, and then bring to the boil, stirring.

Cover the pan with the lid, turn the heat right down, and cook for roughly 15 minutes, or until the rice is cooked and the water absorbed. You will be amazed at how little heat is required, if you have a tight-fitting lid.

Once cooked, remove the lid and fluff up with a spoon or fork, stir in the Parmesan and serve.

This dish is a bit of a mish-mash, but it's very satisfying to eat, and is a great way to start the day when you're out in the fresh air.

Breakfast Hash

SERVES 2 • **PREPARATION TIME** 15 MINUTES • **COOKING TIME** 20 MINUTES

2 rashers streaky bacon, *chopped into 2cm pieces*

2 small sausages, *chopped into 2cm pieces*

½ small onion, *roughly chopped*

4 mushrooms, *quartered*

2 hard-boiled eggs, *roughly chopped*

2 tomatoes, *roughly chopped*

2 slices cold toast, *cut into 2cm pieces*

tea or coffee, to serve

Heat a large frying pan, then add the streaky bacon and cook for 3 minutes until the fat runs. Add the sausages and onions and cook for 10 minutes to brown everything well, then add the mushrooms and cook for a further 3–4 minutes.

Remove from the heat, add the chopped eggs, tomatoes and toast and spoon through lightly.

Serve straight away with tea or coffee - outside one-pan breakfast doesn't get any better.

An easy tomato stew with a good smoked sausage kick. Any sausage will do, but I like to make this with Polish kabanos which are increasingly available nowadays in most supermarkets.

And if you're in a hurry you don't need to cook the onion and garlic first, just add all the ingredients and gently simmer. You'll be pleasantly surprised by the results.

Sweet Tomato and Smoked Polish Sausage Stew

SERVES 2 • PREPARATION TIME 10 MINUTES • COOKING TIME 10–15 MINUTES

2 tbsp vegetable oil or 2 sachets
   mayonnaise
1 small onion, *roughly chopped*
2 garlic cloves, *chopped*
1 tsp dried oregano
1 small glass red wine, optional
1 vegetable stock cube
400g can chopped tomatoes in juice
2 tbsp tomato purée, optional
2 tbsp vinegar (any type will do)
350g smoked Polish kabanos,
   roughly chopped
salt and cracked black peppercorns
bread sticks or flour tortillas, to serve

Heat the oil or mayonnaise in a large pan, add the onions and garlic, and cook for 5 minutes.

Add the remaining ingredients to the pan (except the seasoning and bread) along with a large glass of water. Cook over a low heat until thickened – this will take about 10 minutes.

Season well with salt and cracked black pepper and serve with breadsticks or flour tortillas.

This speedy supper packs a sweet and sour flavour punch. I like to use chicken thigh meat as it is tastier than breast meat, it's also cheaper, and is perfect for this dish.

Sautéed Chicken with Lime, Peppers, Mango and Coriander

SERVES 4 • PREPARATION TIME 10 MINUTES • COOKING TIME 10–15 MINUTES

1 tbsp vegetable oil

4 chicken thighs, *boned*

1 small onion, *finely chopped*

2 tbsp mango chutney

4 tbsp roughly chopped coriander

280g jar chargrilled red and yellow peppers, *well drained and roughly chopped*

juice of 2 large limes

salt and freshly ground black pepper

natural yogurt and flour tortillas, to serve

Heat the oil in a non-stick medium frying pan over a high heat.

Meanwhile cut the thigh meat, including the skin, into 2cm pieces. Place in the hot pan and season well with salt and pepper. Cook over a high heat, stirring occasionally, until the chicken starts to take on a little colour.

Add the onion and cook for 6–7 minutes, or until the chicken is just cooked through.

Add the mango chutney, coriander, peppers and lime juice and stir well.

Serve with yogurt and flour tortillas.

With just a few simple ingredients such as sun-blush tomatoes (see left), you can throw together a fab one-pan meal - enjoy with a salad and some crusty bread.

Turkey and Sun-blush Tomato Tortilla

SERVES 2–4 • PREPARATION TIME 10 MINUTES • COOKING TIME 10 MINUTES

4 tbsp vegetable oil

1 red onion, *roughly sliced*

200g wafer thin turkey, *roughly chopped*

200g sun-blush or sun-dried tomatoes, *roughly chopped*

6 medium eggs

150g blue cheese (stilton, Danish blue or gorgonzola)

salt and freshly ground black pepper

salad leaves and crusty bread, to serve

Heat the oil in a large frying pan, with a lid on. Add the onion and cook for 5–6 minutes until it starts to take on a little colour.

Add the turkey and tomatoes and warm through for a couple of minutes.

Meanwhile, crack the eggs into the pan, break them up with a fork, then add a little pepper and salt. Mix well and quickly as the egg will start to coagulate. Stir for 30 seconds over a fairly high heat, as the egg starts to cook, then turn the heat right down.

Crumble the cheese over the egg, then cover with the lid and leave for 10 minutes with the heat on low. The steam from the eggs will cook the tortilla perfectly and melt the cheese.

Serve straight from the pan with a few salad leaves and crusty bread.

Velveting is a process used to prevent delicate foods like chicken breasts or prawns from overcooking. The food is coated with a mixture of unbeaten egg white, cornflour and sometimes salt and either a touch of sesame or vegetable oil. Velveting keeps the food moist and gives it a smooth texture, hence the name.

This is simple, tasty, one pot cooking at its best.

Light Velvety Chicken and Prawn Soup with Lettuce and Mushrooms

SERVES 2 • PREPARATION TIME 15 MINUTES • COOKING TIME 10–12 MINUTES

2 egg medium whites

3 tbsp cornflour

2 tbsp vegetable oil

2 boneless, skinless chicken breasts, *cut into 2cm pieces*

1 chicken stock cube

1 small onion, *chopped*

1 tbsp finely chopped fresh ginger

100g mushrooms, *finely sliced*

3 tbsp soy sauce, optional

200g frozen cooked prawns

a handful of any lettuce leaves, pak choy or spinach, *finely shredded*

salt and freshly ground black pepper

Place the egg whites in a bowl and break them up slightly with a fork. Add the cornflour, a pinch of salt and a pinch of pepper and the oil, then mix well. Add the chicken and stir to coat.

Place 800ml water, the stock cube, onion, ginger, mushrooms and soy sauce (if using), into a medium pan and place on the hob. Heat until simmering, then cook for 1 minute.

Drop the chicken pieces, one by one into the simmering stock, and then add the frozen prawns. Stir and simmer for 5 minutes, until the prawns are defrosted and the chicken is just cooked. Do not overcook or the chicken and prawns will be tough.

Add the finely shredded lettuce, pak choy or spinach and taste. Adjust the seasoning if necessary.

This is a nice, simple broth that can be cooked while setting up the tent, van or caravan, or simply mucking about with the kids. A splash of cream will give it a creamy finish, but I've left it as an optional extra as it's something else to buy, carry and keep cool.

Simple Pork, Leek and Sage Broth

SERVES 2 • PREPARATION TIME 10 MINUTES • COOKING TIME 1½ HOURS

30g butter, *softened*

30g flour

500g pork shoulder, *cubed*

2 small onions, *roughly chopped*

1 small leek, *roughly chopped and thoroughly washed*

2 garlic cloves, *roughly chopped*

1 small bunch sage, *roughly chopped*

1 chicken stock cube

250g small new potatoes

4–5 tbsp thick cream, optional

salt and freshly ground black pepper

Mix the butter and flour together in a small bowl to form a smooth paste.

Next, place the pork, onions, leek, garlic, sage, stock cube, new potatoes and seasoning in a medium pan. Pour over enough cold water to cover everything by 3cm. Bring to the boil and gently simmer for 1½ hours.

Once the pork is really tender, break off very small pieces of the flour and butter paste and stir it into the simmering broth. The mixture will thicken fairly quickly – don't be tempted to over-thicken it.

Leave it to simmer for a minute or so, then add the cream, if using, for a luxury finish. Season again and serve.

Not the sort of dish you would expect to cook on a camping stove, but this is very easy to prepare and cook, and proves that classic restaurant dishes can be cooked outside using the minimum of equipment. Serve simply with boil-in-the-bag rice (easy for camping!) or crusty bread (even easier!).

Beef Stroganoff

SERVES 4 • **PREPARATION TIME** 15 MINUTES • **COOKING TIME** 15–20 MINUTES

2 tbsp olive oil

1 small onion, *finely chopped*

1 clove garlic, *crushed*

200g chestnut mushrooms, *sliced*

100ml or a small glass of brandy
    or sherry

2 tbsp paprika

300ml double cream

½ beef stock cube

225g fillet steak, *cut into thin strips*

4–6 small gherkins, *sliced and cut into
    fine strips*

small bunch fresh parsley, *chopped,
    optional*

freshly ground black pepper

boil-in-the-bag rice or crusty bread,
    to serve

Heat the oil in a medium pan, with a lid, then add the onion and garlic and cook for 5–6 minutes, to soften slightly.

Add the mushrooms and brandy or sherry and bring to the boil. Cook until the mushrooms have softened, about 3–4 minutes.

Add the paprika, cream, crumbled stock cube and a little black pepper, and bring to the boil until nice and thick.

Drop in the steak strips, then turn off the heat, cover and leave for 5 minutes. This way the steak cooks through, but will still be pink in the middle.

When cooked, add the gherkins and parsley, season with a little more pepper and mix well.

A delicious, sweet treat to enjoy with a cup of tea. I have given measured weights – so you can either weigh the dry ingredients out before you leave home and pop them in a plastic bag. Or you can just add enough flour to the other batter ingredients until you have a thickish batter if that's easier. The secret is to not overwork the batter, or the gluten in the flour will make the scones tough and chewy.

I like to serve these topped with damson jam but any jam will work well.

Warm Buttermilk Pan Scones with Clotted Cream and Jam

SERVES 4 • PREPARATION TIME 10 MINUTES • COOKING TIME 3–4 MINUTES

185g (about 12 tbsp) self-raising flour
1 heaped tsp baking powder
50g (about 4 tbsp) caster sugar
1 medium egg
284ml carton buttermilk
oil, for frying
pinch of salt
clotted cream and jam, to serve

Place the flour, baking powder, sugar and a pinch of salt in a bowl and mix well.

Add the egg and about three-quarters of the buttermilk to the dry ingredients. Mix to a smooth batter – it should be consistency of very thick cream. Add a little more buttermilk if the mixture is too thick.

Heat a non-stick frying pan, add 1 teaspoon of oil and swirl it around.

Carefully spoon 4 small rounds of batter into the pan. Gently cook until the top starts to bubble and is just set. Flip over carefully and cook for 1 minute more. Repeat to use the remaining batter.

Serve warm with topped with clotted cream and jam.

This is a simple boozy dessert that works well using any soft fruit really. Don't overcook the fruit though – it's just a warm-through job.

Poached Plums and Blackberries with Brandy and Brown Sugar

SERVES 2–4 • **PREPARATION TIME** 10 MINUTES • **COOKING TIME** 10 MINUTES

8 large ripe plums

4 tbsp white sugar

2 tbsp salted butter

4 tbsp brandy or any spirit-based
   alcohol

juice of 1 orange

200g blackberries

crisp biscuits such as biscotti,
   to serve

If the plums are ripe enough, slice them lengthways, and remove the stones.

Heat a large frying pan, with a lid. Then add the sugar – it will start to turn brown almost immediately if the pan is hot enough. Once all the sugar has turned brown, or nearly brown, add the butter – it will foam really quickly. Stir well.

Add the alcohol; be very careful if you are using a gas stove as it may ignite from the burner. Stir really well, add the orange juice and bring together to form a nice sauce.

Add the halved or whole plums, cover with the lid and simmer gently for 2 minutes. The skins will start to split from the plums.

At this point add the blackberries and swirl through the sauce to warm through, do not overcook them. Serve warm with the biscuits.

Chapter 4
DUTCH OVEN COOKING

The Dutch oven is a method of outdoor cooking that dates back hundreds of years. It originates from Holland, hence the name – the Dutch took it with them wherever they went in the world. The oven consists of a large cooking pot, traditionally made of cast iron but more likely to be aluminium nowadays. The clever design includes a lid with a deep rim that can hold hot coals or charcoal, so it can heat food from the top as well, like an oven.

I bought my Dutch oven online and use it all the time. It's about 45cm in diameter and about 15cm deep, and has three short legs to raise it above the fire source. You can also buy a version with a handle, so you can suspend it from a tripod over a wood fire.

Dutch ovens are great for cooking for a crowd and are ideal for stews and other one-pot dishes. I've also found that you can warm bread on top of the coals on the lid – a handy tip!

How to prepare your Dutch oven for cooking

The Dutch oven is pretty much failsafe – the only problem you may have is the pan getting too hot, so make sure you do not overload the fire with charcoal or wood. You will be surprised how stable and easy this way of cooking is after a little practice.

If you have access to a recessed fire, as shown in the picture on the preceding page, you won't need to dig a hole!

STEP ONE You will need to dig a hole in the ground big enough to hold the oven with a good 20cm gap around the edge. This is for two reasons – it lets air get to the fuel, and also means it's easier to lift hot coals onto the lid of the pot during cooking.

STEP TWO Build a fire in the hole, light the charcoal or wood and leave until they have turned nice and grey. This will take about 20 minutes. I test the temperature by placing my hand over the hot charcoal and counting. If you can get to five, then it's fine. Any less and it's too hot; any more and it's too cool.

STEP THREE Place the bottom part of the oven onto the fire. The three legs will suspend it slightly above the coals and nestle in nicely. It will not take long to heat the pan ready for cooking. When cooking paella, fruit bread or a tray bake make sure the heat is very low, or they will burn before they are cooked.

STEP FOUR When you are happy to leave the contents of the pot to cook, put the lid on and top with a few coals.

These polpettini or mini meatballs can be made at home and then cooked while you're out. There's no need to sauté anything here, just get straight on and combine all the ingredients for the sauce - the flavour will be fine. Then all you need to do is gently poach the polpettini in the tomatoes and olives.

If you can, use mince from turkey thigh meat as it has more flavour, but any turkey mince will work.

Polpettini with Tomato, Black Olive and Basil Sauce

SERVES 4 • PREPARATION TIME 15 MINUTES • COOKING TIME 20–25 MINUTES

For the polpettini

600g turkey mince

1 small onion, *finely chopped*

1 garlic clove

1 medium egg

finely grated zest and juice of
    1 large lemon

salt and freshly ground black pepper

For the sauce

1 small onion, *finely chopped*

2 x 400g cans chopped tomatoes

150g pitted black olives

3 tsp sugar

dash of any vinegar

1 vegetable stock cube

4 tbsp roughly chopped fresh basil

pitta bread, to serve

Mix the mince well with the onion, the garlic, egg, lemon zest and juice and seasoning. Form the mixture into small balls, each the size of a walnut.

Heat the base of the Dutch oven over the coals. Add the onion, tomatoes, olives, sugar, vinegar and a dash of water. Crumble in the stock cube and bring to the boil. Cook for 5 minutes, stirring occasionally.

Add the meat balls, and coat in the sauce. Cover with the Dutch oven lid, pile on a few coals and gently simmer for a further 15 minutes.

Stir in the basil, season again to taste and serve with torn pitta bread.

Stinging nettles work really well when stewed lightly with stock and vegetables – they give this dish a pungent flavour. Take care when picking them, it can be a tricky task! Make sure you wear protective gloves and wash the leaves really well. The best time of year to pick nettles is from spring to early winter. If you can't get hold of them, use spinach, watercress or rocket instead.

Pot Roast Poussin with Nettles and Sweet Potatoes

SERVES 4 • PREPARATION TIME 15 MINUTES • COOKING TIME ABOUT 45 MINUTES–1 HOUR

4 x poussin or 2 x 650g medium chickens or game hens

50g unsalted butter

1 large onion, *finely chopped*

1 small sweet potato, *finely diced*

1 garlic clove, *finely chopped*

1 large bunch stinging nettle leaves, spinach, watercress or rocket

10–12 fresh sage leaves, *finely chopped*

2–3 tsp caster sugar

1 chicken stock cube

salt and freshly ground black pepper

Season the birds all over with salt and pepper.

Heat the butter in the Dutch oven base until it is bubbling. When the butter is starting to brown, add the birds and brown them all over.

Add the onion, sweet potato and garlic and cook for 3–5 minutes so they take on a little colour.

Add the nettles, sage, sugar and crumbled stock cube and stir well. Bring to the boil, place the lid on and pile a few hot coals on top of the oven. Cook for 45 minutes to 1 hour, occasionally basting the birds with the cooking liquid. The slower you cook the dish, the better.

When cooked, leave to cool for 20 minutes before eating.

Not really authentic, I know, but it's pretty tasty all the same. You will need a very cool fire here or the rice will cook too quickly.

Cheat's Paella

SERVES 4 AS A MAIN COURSE OR 8 AS A STARTER • PREPARATION TIME 15 MINUTES • COOKING TIME 20 MINUTES

4 tbsp olive oil

2 small onions, *finely chopped*

3 garlic cloves, *finely chopped*

1 red pepper, *cut into 1cm pieces*

1 tsp smoked paprika

350g long grain rice

2 skinned and boned chicken thighs,
    cut into thick strips

500g bag frozen mixed seafood,
    including squid, mussels and
    chunks of meaty fish

600ml boiling water

1 vegetable stock cube

3 tbsp tomato purée

2 heaped tbsp roughly chopped
    fresh parsley

salt and freshly ground black pepper

Heat the oil in the Dutch oven and then add the onions, garlic and red pepper. Cook for 10 minutes so that the pepper releases its colour slightly –add half a teaspoon of paprika to help that along.

Add the rice and stir well to coat it in the oil and onion mix. Add the chicken pieces, seafood and remaining paprika and mix really well. Next, add the boiling water, stock cube, tomato purée and seasoning and stir thoroughly.

Bring back to a slow boil, then cover with the lid. Add a few hot coals to the top and cook for about 15 minutes, then check to make sure all the liquid has been absorbed.

Add the parsley and stir well. Re-cover and leave for 10 minutes off the heat. That's it – really easy!

Kedgeree is a marvellous dish and a great old English favourite. This is a very easy twist on the classic version.

I use packets of frozen cooked rice here, I take them out of the freezer, put them in a cool box, along with the defrosted prawns and take them with me – really handy!

Quick Crab, Prawn and Mushroom Kedgeree with Boiled Eggs and Parsley

SERVES 2 • PREPARATION TIME 15 MINUTES • COOKING TIME 10–15 MINUTES

50g unsalted butter, *finely diced*
225g baby button mushrooms, *halved*
4 spring onions, *chopped*
200g frozen cooked rice
170g can crabmeat, *drained*
250g frozen cooked prawns, *defrosted and drained*
4 tbsp roughly chopped fresh parsley
2 hard-boiled eggs, *shelled and roughly chopped*
salt and freshly ground black pepper

Heat half the butter in the Dutch oven. Add the mushrooms and spring onions to the pan and cook for 2–3 minutes. Add the rice and heat it through thoroughly, stirring to prevent it from sticking.

Stir in the crabmeat, prawns, parsley and the remaining butter. Finally, add the chopped eggs and season well with salt and pepper. Serve straight away.

Coat the chicken and pop it in an airtight lidded container before you head out and all the hard work is done! Then you just need to cook it and throw a few ingredients in the pan to finish it off – perfect!

Fried Chicken with Parmesan Cheese and Pine Nuts

SERVES 4 • **PREPARATION TIME** 20 MINUTES • **COOKING TIME** 25–35 MINUTES

8 skinned and boned chicken thighs

6 tbsp plain flour

300ml milk

4 tbsp vegetable oil or 4 small
   sachets of mayonnaise

50g unsalted butter

½ chicken stock cube

finely grated zest and juice of
   2 large lemons

100g pine nuts

6 tbsp chopped fresh parsley

75g Parmesan cheese, *roughly grated*

salt and freshly ground black pepper

Season the chicken thighs well with salt and pepper. Place the flour into a large bowl and the milk into another. Dip the chicken into the flour, then the milk, then back into the flour. Repeat until all the chicken is coated. Set aside in an airtight lidded container in the fridge until ready to cook.

Heat the oil or mayonnaise and the butter until bubbling in the Dutch oven base, and slightly browned. Add the chicken and cook over a moderate heat on both sides for 12–15 minutes, or until cooked through, then carefully remove and place on a plate or tray.

Add 1 mug of water, the crumbled stock cube and lemon zest and juice to the pan. Bring to the boil, scraping the bottom of the pan. Simmer the liquid until it is roughly reduced by half. Return the chicken to the pan and heat through until piping hot.

Serve the chicken sprinkled with the pine nuts, parsley and cheese.

Having cooked at the home of Tex-Mex in San Antonio, Texas, this recipe is rather different from the versions we have in Europe. The colour and flavour of Texan chilli is really important and it has many ingredients to enhance both, including cumin and paprika.

The sauce should be almost like a very thick soup, with less meat than we are used to. I find mince with a 20 per cent fat content works best for this chilli.

Tex-Mex Black-eyed Bean Chilli

SERVE 4–6 • PREPARATION TIME 15 MINUTES • COOKING TIME 40–50 MINUTES

1 tbsp vegetable oil

2 large onions, *finely chopped*

2 garlic cloves, *finely chopped*

500g beef mince

1 tsp ground cumin

1 tsp ground cinnamon

1 tsp paprika, optional

½ tsp dried chilli flakes

1 tsp dried oregano

400g can chopped tomatoes

2 tbsp tomato purée

2 tsp sugar

400g can black-eyed beans, *drained*

salt and freshly ground black pepper

Cornbread Muffins (see page 215),
  to serve, optional

Heat the oil in the Dutch oven and add the onions and garlic. Cook gently until they start to soften.

Add the mince and break up well with a wooden spoon. Cook the meat until all the moisture has evaporated and it is starting to brown nicely.

Next add the spices, oregano, tomatoes, tomato purée, sugar and 300ml water. Mix well and season with salt and pepper. Finally add the drained beans and cook gently for 30–40 minutes.

Serve with cornbread, if liked, and tuck in.

I love hot pot! I once cooked this on the side of Glencoe, a mountain pass in Scotland, for an advert, and the crew really loved it. You won't get the traditional crispy potato top, but you will get a delicious tasty meal. If the fire is too hot then slide the oven to one side until the heat has gone from the charcoal or coals.

Really Easy Tasty Mince Hotpot

SERVES 6–8 • PREPARATION TIME 15 MINUTES • COOKING TIME 40–50 MINUTES

4 tbsp vegetable oil

2 small onions, *chopped*

200g mushrooms, *thickly sliced*

500g beef or lamb mince

2 tbsp plain flour

400g can chopped tomatoes

1 beef stock cube

2–3 sachets or 3 tbsp brown sauce

5 large potatoes, *chopped into 3cm chunks*

salt and freshly ground black pepper

Add half the vegetable oil to the base of the Dutch oven. Add the onions and mushrooms and cook over a high heat for 10 minutes.

Add the mince, break up well with a wooden spoon, and cook until it changes colour from red to a fawny-brown colour, stirring occasionally.

Stir in the flour, tomatoes, 100ml water, the crumbled stock cube and brown sauce and mix really well.

Toss the chopped potatoes in a large bowl with a little salt and pepper and the remaining vegetable oil. Pile the potatoes on to the bubbling mixture, cover and add a few coals to the top of the oven. Cook for 20–30 minutes.

I have cooked this dish for many years – it's so simple and has a wonderful flavour. If you mix the spices and the herby yogurt before you go, this makes it much easier when you are ready to cook.

This makes an ideal starter for 4 or a main course for 2.

Simple Moroccan Turkey Stew

SERVES 2 • PREPARATION TIME 15 MINUTES • COOKING TIME 25 MINUTES

For the herby yogurt

3 tbsp chopped fresh parsley

3 tbsp chopped fresh mint

3 tbsp chopped fresh coriander

200g thick natural yogurt

1 tbsp clear honey

For the stew

2 tbsp vegetable oil

2 garlic cloves, *finely chopped*

1 small onion, *chopped finely*

250g turkey mince

1 heaped tsp ground cumin

1 tsp ground cinnamon

pinch of chilli powder

1 tbsp plain flour

1 chicken stock cube

salt and freshly ground black pepper

In an airtight lidded container mix the yogurt with half the chopped herbs and the honey.

Heat the vegetable oil in the Dutch oven and add the garlic and onions. Cook over a low heat to soften.

Add the turkey mince spices, flour and seasoning and mix well. Add 400ml water and crumble over the chicken stock cube, stir until simmering, then cook for 15 minutes, stirring occasionally, as the flour may make it catch slightly. The stew should thicken slightly due to the flour.

When ready, check the seasoning, then add the remaining herbs and serve with the yogurt.

Fresh or canned pineapple works well in this pud. Don't be put off by the chilli – it lifts the flavour of the pineapple to give it a little kick! Other canned fruit works just as well as the pineapple.

Warm Chilli Pineapple with Fromage Frais

SERVES 4–6 • PREPARATION TIME 10 MINUTES • COOKING TIME 5–10 MINUTES

2 tsp finely chopped fresh red chilli

250g granulated sugar

1 medium-sized fresh pineapple,
  skinned and sliced into 1cm slices or
  400g can pineapple rings in syrup,
  well drained

2 tsp butter

freshly ground black pepper

vanilla fromage frais, natural yogurt
  or crème fraîche, to serve

Place the chilli, sugar and 400ml water in the Dutch oven base. Bring to the boil and simmer for 1 minute.

Dust the pineapple slices with a little black pepper. Pop the seasoned pineapple slices into the pan and warm through for 1–2 minutes. Then add the butter and mix in well.

Carefully spoon the pineapple into warm bowls, add a little of the chilli syrup, and top with a large spoonful of vanilla fromage frais, natural yogurt or crème fraîche.

One of the most famous foods to come out of Ireland is soda bread. It's made in all sorts of different ways but I think one of the best is to use stout to help the dough rise and give the bread an unusual colour and flavour.

This bread really has to be eaten on the same day you make it – it's delicious served buttered with a slice of mature Cheddar and a glass of the black stuff!

Fruit and Stout Soda Bread

MAKES 1 X 23CM ROUND LOAF • PREPARATION TIME 15 MINUTES • COOKING TIME 15–20 MINUTES

oil, for greasing

250g malted flour

100g strong plain flour

110g demerara sugar

3 heaped tbsp bicarbonate of soda

3 good pinches of sea salt

150g mixed dried fruit such as sultanas, currants or cranberries

1 medium egg, *beaten*

4 tbsp olive oil

150ml stout

butter and slices of mature Cheddar cheese, to serve

Heat plenty of coals or charcoal until they are all grey.

Spread the hot coals or charcoal out with a stick to the size of the base of the oven. Place the Dutch oven directly on to the coals, and place an inverted 23cm Victoria sandwich tin in the oven. Lightly oil the base of the tray, which will be facing up – you will be using this as a surface to cook on. Place the lid on the Dutch oven and let it heat up.

Next, place the flours, sugar, bicarbonate of soda, salt and fruit into a bowl. Add the egg, olive oil and enough stout to make a soft dough. Mould the dough into a ball and then flatten it slightly.

Pop the flattened ball of dough on to the inverted oiled tin, then using a sharp knife score a cross across the top of the dough. Cover the Dutch oven with the lid, place a few coals or charcoal on top and bake until the bread is risen and nicely browned, this will probably take 15–20 minutes depending on the heat of the oven and coals.

Set aside to cool. Break into chunks and serve with the butter and Cheddar plus a glass or two of stout to drink.

Chapter 5
COOKING ON A WOOD FIRE

I'm more than happy to cook all year round using any method, but the wood fire has to come top as you can huddle round it for warmth as well. My daughter and I have spent many contented hours cooking bacon and eggs over an open fire.

I have tried to keep the ingredients lists in the following recipes nice and tight, so you are not lugging too much kit about. I generally stick to one or two pans maximum; one with a tight-fitting lid is always very handy. Add to that a wooden spoon, tongs and knife and fork and you're ready to go.

Another good tip is to collect those individually sealed sachets of salt, pepper and sugar you find in takeaway restaurants. These are really handy for campfire cooking and I have found that you can even sauté onions and pieces of meat quite happily in two or three small sachets of mayonnaise – yes it's true, try it!

How to build a wood fire

You can of course take the Ray Mears approach, using flints or a couple of dry sticks and piece of leather. I tend to use more up-to-date methods!

Before you build your fire, check the direction of the wind. This is for two reasons; firstly, you don't want smoke blowing over the eating area, and secondly, if you light the fire on the up-wind side, the wind will then blow into the branches and sticks, lighting them all quicker.

Another important note: if you are not on your own land, always get the owner's permission before building an open fire.

SAFETY

I tend to cook a lot more on an open fire in the winter months, because in the warmer months there's a risk of setting a piece of ground alight as everything is so dry. However, a fire that is well contained with large bricks or stones is fine, provided you keep an eye on it and put it out with plenty of water once finished.

STEP ONE Get your materials ready, whether you are chopping your own wood or gathering kindling.

STEP TWO Arrange kindling such as old newspapers, straw and very small dry twigs in a small heap to get the fire started.

STEP THREE Once the fire is going add larger twigs in a wig-wam style, so the air can get into the wood and get the fire going – essential on wet days. I then always make sure I have seasoned, dry branches or split dry logs to hand.

For pure laziness I sometimes use a portable gas bottle and torch, this is perfect in the middle of winter to get large fires going from sodden wet wood.

STEP FOUR When all the wood has burnt down and you have a nice pile of greying ashes and embers, it's time to start cooking.

I once filmed in San Antonio, Texas, and was given tacos for lunch. I was expecting the crispy version that we get here in the UK, but to my surprise they were the soft wrapped variety – here is my nod to that trip.

Warm Mixed Mushroom Tacos with Chilli and Mature Cheddar

SERVES 4–6 • PREPARATION TIME 10 MINUTES • COOKING TIME 10–15 MINUTES

4 tbsp olive oil

1 small onion, *roughly chopped*

2 tsp finely chopped fresh red chilli

3 garlic cloves, *chopped*

2 tsp chopped fresh oregano

500g mixed mushrooms eg wild, flat, brown cap and portabello, *roughly chopped*

225g mature Cheddar cheese, *roughly grated*

200ml soured cream plus extra to serve

2 tbsp fresh chopped coriander, plus extra to serve

4–6 small soft flour tortillas

salt and freshly ground black pepper

fresh lime wedges, to serve

Heat half the oil in a large pan or wok, and add the onion, chilli, garlic and oregano, cook until the onion has softened, stirring occasionally. Remove from the wok and place in a bowl.

Heat the remaining olive oil in the pan and add the mushrooms. Cook over a high heat (the hotter the better) until softened, try to singe the mushrooms.

Spoon the mushrooms into the bowl with the onions. Add the cheese, soured cream and coriander, then season generously and stir well.

Immediately divide the mixture among the soft tortillas, roll up and serve with the extra soured cream, coriander and wedges of fresh lime.

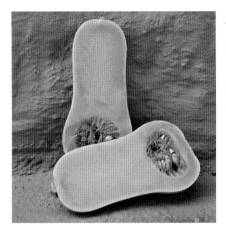

Try this in the autumn when butternut squash is in season – it's really tasty as a starter or dip with glass of something cold.

I sometimes add more unusual ingredient to my recipes – here a splash or two of lager adds a hoppy note that works really well with the squash.

Butternut Squash Hash with Red Onions, Chilli, Garlic and Beer

SERVES 4 • PREPARATION TIME 15 MINUTES • COOKING TIME 25–30 MINUTES

4 tbsp olive oil

2 small red onions, *roughly chopped*

2 garlic cloves, *roughly chopped*

2 tsp roughly chopped fresh red chilli

1 butternut squash, peeled, *seeded and roughly chopped*

150ml light beer, e.g. lager (or use water)

1 vegetable stock cube

1 tsp sugar

salt and freshly ground black pepper

crackers or crispy tortillas, to serve

Heat the oil in a frying pan and add the onions, garlic, chilli and squash. Season really well and cook for 15 minutes, until the vegetables have a little colour.

Add the beer (or water), crumble over the stock cube and add the sugar. Bring to a simmer and cook until the squash starts to fall apart on the outside edges. At this point, gently break the squash up until you have a thick stew-like consistency, but don't go mad.

Season again to taste and serve warm with crackers or crispy tortillas.

This is a simple recipe, (especially if you ask your fishmonger to prepare the fish for you) packed full of flavour and colour. You'll be surprised how little orange juice you will need to make a lovely sauce. Just remember not to overcook the fish.

Chop-cut Bass with Green Peppercorns, Dill and Orange Butter

SERVES 4 • **PREPARATION TIME** 20 MINUTES • **COOKING TIME** 10 MINUTES

2 x 350g bass, gutted, *scaled and heads and fins removed*

4 tbsp olive oil

2 tbsp plain flour or cornflour

zest and juice of 1 large orange

½ fish stock cube

140g butter, *roughly chopped*

2 tsp green peppercorns in brine plus 2 tsp of the brine

small bunch of fresh dill, *chopped*

salt and freshly ground black pepper

crusty bread, to serve

Before you leave home, cut each fish in half from where the top fin was to the open cavity where the guts were.

Heat a frying pan over the fire until it is nice and hot. Add the oil to the pan.

Generously season the fish inside and out. Dust each piece of fish with a little flour. Pop the fish in the pan and cook it for 3–4 minutes on each side.

Once the fish is cooked, add the orange zest and juice, crumbled stock cube, butter, green peppercorns and brine to the pan. Bring to the boil and coat the fish well – the sauce will reduce and thicken as the orange juice evaporates. Once thickened slightly, add the dill and stir well.

Serve straight from the pan with crusty bread.

I have been very fortunate over the years to have caught a few wild brown trout. I have a friend who catches many more than I do and is always delivering them to me, so it made ideal sense to add a recipe to the campfire cooking section. I have cooked this recipe many times – it also works very well with small rainbow trout if you cannot get hold of wild fish.

Whole Brown Trout with Black Pepper, Brown Butter and Lemon

SERVES 2 • PREPARATION TIME 15 MINUTES • COOKING TIME 10 MINUTES

2 x 225g wild brown or rainbow trout, *gutted and heads removed*

4 tbsp unsalted butter, *roughly chopped*

juice of 2 large lemons

½ tsp black peppercorns, *cracked*

salt

brown bread and lemon wedges, to serve

Wash the trout well and dry with kitchen paper.

Heat a frying pan over the fire, taking care not to let it get too hot, then add the butter and heat until it is just foaming.

Season the fish well inside and out with salt only. Place into the foaming butter and cook for 4–5 minutes, then flip over and cook again for 4–5 minutes. The fish will be very slightly undercooked on the bone.

Add the lemon juice and cracked black pepper and swirl all the juices together, then spoon them over the fish. That's it – serve straight from the pan with chunks of brown bread.

This sounds strange I know, but the addition of a little condensed milk really makes a big difference to the end flavour of this fried chicken. This, coupled with the tanginess of the Bramley apple, makes a great combination.

Before you leave home, breadcrumb the chicken, and make up the dressing, then all you have to do while you are out is prepare and mix the salad.

Sweet Fried Chicken with Tangy Apple and Pear Salad

SERVES 4 • PREPARATION TIME 40–50 MINUTES • COOKING TIME 15–20 MINUTES

For the chicken

4 skinned and boned chicken thighs

2 tbsp Dijon mustard

4 tbsp condensed milk

3 tbsp plain flour

2 medium eggs, *lightly beaten*

10–12 tbsp dried breadcrumbs

4 tbsp vegetable oil

For the salad

grated zest and juice of 2 large limes

1 tbsp cider vinegar

3 tsp caster sugar

4 tbsp extra virgin olive oil

1 tbsp Dijon mustard

2 dessert apples, e.g. Cox's

1 large Bramley apple

2 ripe Conference pears

½ iceberg lettuce, *shredded*

salt and freshly ground black pepper

Place the chicken thighs in a shallow dish and spread the mustard and condensed milk over them. Set aside for 20–30 minutes.

Place the flour, beaten egg and breadcrumbs into three separate wide, shallow dishes. Lightly dust the coated chicken thighs in a little flour, then dip into beaten egg and finally the breadcrumbs, patting down well. Transfer to an airtight lidded container and pop in the fridge until you are ready to head out.

To make the dressing, place the lime zest, juice, vinegar, sugar, olive oil, mustard and seasoning in a screw-top jar with a lid, and give it a good shake to mix well.

When you are ready to cook, heat a large frying pan, then add the vegetable oil. Place the crumbed thighs into the hot oil, and cook for 8–10 minutes on each side, nice and gently – you may need a little longer.

Next, roughly grate the apples, with skin, discarding the cores, and place in a large bowl. Quarter the pears and remove the cores, then slice finely and add to the bowl. Pour over the dressing and mix well to coat. Next add the lettuce and mix the salad together. To serve, place some salad on a plate and top with a chicken thigh.

When I was a young chef, boiled chicken was always on the menu. Generally speaking it was an older fowl, such as a capon (the name for a castrated cockerel) or an older chicken. Today you very rarely see dishes made with older fowl so I have adapted this delicious dish for the campfire. Here I'm using leg joints rather than a whole bird purely because it's quicker and slightly cheaper. For me, the only sauce to serve with this dish is a flavoured mayo-based dip – roast garlic fits the bill perfectly. The garlic should be roasted in the conventional oven before you go out – alternatively, you can now buy very good ready-made roasted garlic mayonnaise.

Simmered Chicken with Roasted Garlic Mayo and Onions

SERVES 4 • PREPARATION TIME 10 MINUTES • COOKING TIME 20 MINUTES

1 small garlic bulb

4 chicken legs (skin on)

2 onions, finely sliced

2 carrots, *roughly chopped*

3 sticks celery, *roughly chopped*

1 small leek, *thoroughly washed and roughly chopped*

1 chicken stock cube

250g mayonnaise

4 tbsp chopped fresh parsley

salt and freshly ground black pepper

crusty bread, to serve

Preheat the oven to 200°C/gas mark 6. Cut the whole bulb of garlic in half horizontally and place it cut side down on a non-stick baking tray. Roast the garlic for 20 minutes or until it is very soft and squidgy. Set aside to cool.

Heat the campfire until the wood has burnt down and you have a nice pile of greying ashes and embers.

Place a medium pan on the stand and add the chicken legs. Add the vegetables and cover with cold water. Add the crumbled stock cube and season. Bring to a simmer, cover and cook for 35–40 minutes, or until the legs are cooked.

Meanwhile, mix the roasted garlic pulp and chopped parsley into the mayonnaise and season with black pepper. You can of course do this at home before you leave – all you need to do is to squeeze the cooked garlic from the bulb; it will come out easily, like toothpaste.

Once the chicken is cooked, the skin will come off easily. Carefully remove it and discard – I use a couple of forks for this. Lift out the chicken pieces, and eat dipped in the garlic mayo and with crusty bread. I tend to eat the stock and vegetables with a spoon as soup afterwards. Great one-pot cooking!

Quesadillas are flour tortillas filled with cheese and other ingredients which are then gently fried until they are golden and crisp. These are delicious to eat straight from the pan.

Turkey, Cheddar, Red Onion and Chilli Quesadillas

SERVES 4 • **PREPARATION TIME** 10 MINUTES • **COOKING TIME** 25 MINUTES

2 tbsp olive oil

2 large red onions, *thinly sliced*

1 tbsp chopped fresh red chilli

4 large soft flour tortillas

100g mature Cheddar cheese, *grated*

150g wafer thin cooked ham,
   cut into strips

150g cooked turkey or chicken, *sliced*

2 tbsp chopped fresh coriander

Pickled Corn Rings, to serve (see page
   184), optional

Place half the oil in a large frying pan and heat it over the fire. Add the onion and chilli and fry until soft and golden – about 15 minutes. Transfer to a plate. Wipe out the pan with kitchen paper.

Lay the wraps out on a flat surface and place one quarter of the cheese, ham, turkey or chicken, coriander and onion and chilli, on one half of each wrap. Fold the wrap over, to make a semi-circle.

Heat the frying pan again and brush it lightly with the remaining oil. Place 2 wraps into the pan and cook gently over a medium heat for 1–2 minutes on each side, until golden and crisp. Repeat to cook the remaining wraps.

Serve straight away with Pickled Corn Rings.

Rabbit with Smoked Bacon, Spinach and Red Wine

SERVES 4 • PREPARATION TIME 15 MINUTES (MORE IF YOU ARE JOINTING THE RABBIT) • COOKING TIME 1 HOUR – 1 HOUR 10 MINUTES

The secret here is to joint the rabbit before you go out to cook. It's a bit fiddly, but well worth a go, and relatively simple. The first time it may take you a while, but once you get the hang of it, it does get easier. Alternatively, your butcher or game dealer can do it for you.

You will end up with six nice pieces of meat, plus the rib cage to add flavour to the dish. Once cooked there is a little bit of meat on the rib cage to nibble on but it's not really worth serving as part of the dish. I simmer the legs and shoulders initially then add the loins, as they take far less time to cook.

1 x 750g prepared rabbit

150g smoked streaky bacon, *chopped*

1 glass red wine

1 chicken stock cube

3 tsp sugar

150g baby leaf spinach

1 tbsp cornflour or arrowroot

salt and freshly ground black pepper

To joint the rabbit, place it on a chopping board. Remove the back legs by cutting through the top of the leg where it attaches to the body, then dislocate the leg by breaking the leg towards the body. The leg ball joint will pop out easily. Once out, cut around and free the leg from the body. Repeat with the other leg, then cut each leg into two pieces, through the knee joint. Next, cut the shoulders from the body – there is no ball and socket joint here, just muscle attaching to the rib cage. Finally, cut the loin into 2 pieces with a sharp knife.

Heat a large pan over the fire, making sure it is not too hot. Add the bacon to the pan and stir well, cooking until the bacon is nicely browned and the fat has run out of the cooked bacon. Next, add the rabbit legs, shoulders and rib cage and brown them slightly.

Add the red wine, 1 cup of cold water, the crumbled stock cube, sugar and salt and pepper. Bring to a simmer, then cover with a lid. Gently simmer for 35–40 minutes, or until the meat is cooked and falling away from the bone. Do not overcook or the rabbit will be dry.

Add the two pieces of loin and cover again, cook for a further 15 minutes. The loin can be slightly undercooked, as it will be incredibly tender and juicy. Once you are happy, lift out the rabbit pieces, place them on a plate and cover with a piece of foil.

Add the spinach to the pan, place the lid on and leave to simmer for 2–3 minutes. It will cook down fairly quickly to one quarter of its original volume.

At this point, mix the cornflour or arrowroot with 2 tablespoons of cold water. Add the cornflour paste to the spinach and red wine stock and stir until thickened. Return the rabbit to the pan and re-heat. Season well and serve.

No campfire section would be complete without a game bird dish. The wonderfully tangy flavour comes from the citrus marinade here, and then the bird is gently simmered. Add more or less stock and a little more lime if you want.

I like to buy and cook pheasants from autumn until late winter, when they are at their best and in season.

Marinated Pheasant with Lime and Green Beans

SERVES 2 • **PREPARATION TIME** 15 MINUTES PLUS OVERNIGHT MARINATING • **COOKING TIME** 30 MINUTES

1 small onion, *very finely sliced*
400ml cold chicken stock
3 tbsp clear honey
finely grated zest and juice of
 4 large limes
1 plump, plucked pheasant,
 approximately 350g
handful of green beans,
 roughly chopped
salt and freshly ground black pepper

Place the onion, chicken stock and honey into a shallow dish and mix really well. Then add the lime zest and juice and plenty of seasoning.

Place the pheasant on a chopping board and remove its back bone by cutting down either side of it with a sharp knife. Break the pheasant open and flatten well, then remove the knuckles.

Place the prepared pheasant halves in the marinade and cover with clingfilm. Chill in the fridge overnight.

When you are ready to cook, take the pheasant pieces out of the marinade, dry them very well with kitchen paper, and season well.

Heat a large frying pan over the fire. Spoon all of the marinade into the pan and bring to the boil, simmering for 15 minutes. Next, add the pheasant halves to the pan, along with the beans, and gently simmer for 10 minutes loosely covered with some foil. Carefully turn over and cook for a further 5 minutes.

Serve the pheasant in the broth.

This quick, easy meal looks great and tastes good with a sharp kick from the cabbage. It's also a nice way to cook corn on the cob and makes the kernels much sweeter.

Hamburger Hash with Fresh Sweetcorn and Pickled Cabbage

SERVES 4 • PREPARATION TIME 10 MINUTES • COOKING TIME 15 MINUTES

2 tbsp oil or 2 small sachets of
   mayonnaise
4 x 125g hamburgers, *each one roughly*
   cut into 6 pieces
2 corn on the cob, *halved*
1 garlic clove, *finely chopped*
1 small onion, *roughly chopped*
2–4 tbsp pickled red cabbage or
   chopped gherkins
salt and freshly ground black pepper

Heat the campfire until the wood has burnt down and you have a nice pile of greying ashes and embers.

Place a large frying pan over the heat and add the oil or mayonnaise. Add the hamburger pieces and cook them for 6–7 minutes, or until cooked through and nicely coloured.

There will be a little oil and fat in the pan now. Remove the hamburger pieces and keep them warm, covered with a little foil.

On a chopping board, turn each corn on the cob half on its end and carefully shave off the corn with a sharp knife, so you end up with all the kernels on the board. Add the kernels to the hot fat and oil, along with the garlic, then season well with salt and pepper – you may have to place a lid on as the kernels may pop like popcorn. Cook the corn until it is nicely coloured. Add the onion and cook until it is lightly coloured.

Return the cooked hamburger pieces to the pan and heat through. Finally add the pickled cabbage or gherkins and stir through.

This is one of my favourite ways of cooking sausages outdoors. The vinegar really cuts through the richness of the sausages to give a fantastic flavour. Serve with plenty of crusty bread to mop up the delicious gravy.

Campfire Sausages with Vinegar Onion Gravy

SERVES 4 • PREPARATION TIME 10 MINUTES • COOKING TIME 20 MINUTES

2 tbsp oil or 2 small sachets
   of mayonnaise
8 plump sausages
2 medium onions, *finely sliced*
1 tbsp or 2 small sachets vinegar
1 beef stock cube
1 tbsp cornflour or arrowroot
salt and freshly ground black pepper
crusty bread, to serve

Heat the campfire until the wood has burnt down and you have a nice pile of greying ashes and embers.

Place a large frying pan on the stand over the fire and add the oil or mayonnaise. Heat until it is bubbling slightly.

Prick the sausages lightly, this will stop them from exploding, and place in the pan. Brown the sausages gently all over – don't go mad here, all we want is a nice colour. Once browned, remove with tongs and place on a plate.

Add the onions to the pan and cook them for about 5–10 minutes or until they soften and colour slightly. Add the vinegar to the pan and cook until it has mostly evaporated. Add 400ml water and the crumbled stock cube, season well and bring to the boil. Return the sausages to the pan, cover, then cook for 10 minutes, or until cooked through.

Once the sausages are cooked, mix the cornflour or arrowroot with 1 tablespoon of cold water to form a smooth paste. Gently pour a little paste into the pan and stir it in with the wooden spoon. It should thicken, if the sauce is boiling, straight away. The aim here is to get a nice smooth consistency without it being too thick and gloopy. If you add too much of the paste simply add a little water to thin it out again. Season well and serve with crusty bread.

As you may have realised by now, the secret to all outdoor cooking is to prepare as much as you can before you go. So, make up the meatballs and chill them. Get everything ready for the soup, and you're ready for the off.

Soupy Spicy Lamb Meatballs with Gnocchi and Shiitake Mushrooms

SERVES 4 • PREPARATION TIME 10 MINUTES • COOKING TIME 25 MINUTES

400g minced lamb
½ tsp chilli powder
½ tsp ground nutmeg
½ tsp ground cinnamon
1 medium egg, *beaten*
1 tbsp oil
100g shiitake mushrooms, *thinly sliced*
1 medium onion, *finely chopped*
2 garlic cloves, *crushed*
1 lamb or chicken stock cube
2 tbsp soy sauce
juice of 2 large limes
100g ready-to-eat gnocchi
1 tbsp cornflour or arrowroot
2 tbsp chopped fresh coriander

To make the meatballs, place the lamb, chilli powder, nutmeg, cinnamon, beaten egg and plenty of seasoning into a bowl and mix well. Next form into balls each the size of a small walnut, then chill well.

Heat a large frying pan or wok over the campfire. Add the oil and swirl it around to coat the base of the pan. Add the meatballs and cook until they brown nicely. Once browned, remove them from the pan and place on a plate.

Add the mushrooms, onion, garlic, crumbled stock cube, soy sauce, lime juice and 400ml water to the pan and bring to the boil. Gently simmer for 15 minutes, turning occasionally until cooked.

Add the gnocchi and meatballs to the pan and cook for a further 5–6 minutes.

Mix the cornflour and 2 tablespoons cold water to form a smooth paste, add a little of the paste to the boiling juices and stir until slightly thickened. Season again and serve.

Chapter 6
PICNICS

I thought it would be really nice to write a chapter on picnics that are easy to transport and serve. Yes, I know what you are thinking, all picnics are easy, but what I have tried to do here is to create dishes that are good for a range of outdoor activities. I wanted all the dishes to have a balance of texture, flavour, colour and nutrition. Above all they had to sustain and taste really good. Also, I wanted to come up with dishes that could be made the day before at home, chilled and packed with the minimum of fuss.

For many years I have had and prepared picnic food that while being very good, perhaps needed a bit of upgrading. Once I looked into various ideas the following chapter came together. I love meatloaf, I love 3 beans in any way, shape or form and I also love vegetables that are roasted and given bags of flavour. Here I hope, is fresh approach to picnic food.

This is an update on the classic 70s recipe and makes a delicious, satisfying picnic dish. I like to add a little chopped Bombay mix to the mayo for a little extra crunch. You can also add chopped dried fruit such as white raisins or even cranberries, for a fruity flavour.

Spicy Devilled Eggs

SERVES 4 • PREPARATION TIME 15 MINUTES • COOKING TIME 10–12 MINUTES

8 medium eggs, at room temperature
8 tbsp good-quality mayonnaise
1 heaped tbsp wholegrain mustard
2 spring onions, *very finely chopped*
½ tsp curry powder
½ tsp smoked paprika
few drops of Tabasco sauce
2 tbsp Bombay mix, *roughly chopped*
1 tbsp chopped dried fruit
salt and freshly ground black pepper
watercress, to serve

Bring a pan of water to the boil, then carefully place in the eggs. Bring the water back to the boil, then turn down the heat and allow to simmer for 10–12 minutes.

Using a slotted spoon, carefully lift the eggs out of the pan and place them in a bowl. Place them under cold running water for 10 minutes – this will stop the egg yolk discolouring the cooked white.

Crack and shell each egg and dry them well on kitchen paper. Slice the eggs in half lengthways, and scoop the yolks into a bowl. Slice a thin sliver off the rounded part of the cooked whites so they sit nicely.

Break up the yolks with a fork, then add the mayo, mustard, spring onions, curry, paprika, Tabasco and really mix well. Add a little salt and pepper to taste. At this point add the chopped Bombay mix and fruit. Spoon back into the egg halves, leaving a heaped look.

Pack into an airtight lidded box and chill well. I like to serve mine with plenty of watercress sprigs.

The first time I cooked this on TV it went down really well. Since then it's become part of my repertoire at home.

Cashew and Mushroom Bake

SERVES 6 • PREPARATION TIME 20 MINUTES • COOKING TIME 40-50 MINUTES

vegetable oil, for greasing

2 tbsp olive oil

1 small onion, *chopped*

1 tsp very finely chopped fresh
   red chilli

2 garlic cloves, *crushed*

2 x 400g cans chick peas, *well drained*

200g unsalted cashew nuts,
   roughly chopped

5 thick slices of bread

2 medium eggs, *lightly beaten*

1 tbsp chopped fresh rosemary

1 tbsp fresh oregano

juice of 1 large lemon

200ml vegetable stock

1 tbsp vegetable oil

225g flat mushrooms, *chopped*

salt and freshly ground black pepper

green salad, crusty bread and garlic
   mayo, to serve

Preheat the oven to 200°C/gas mark 6. Oil a 900g loaf tin.

Heat the olive oil in a medium frying pan and gently cook the onion, chilli and garlic for 10 minutes until softened.

Place the chick peas and cashew nuts into a food processor and blitz until fairly smooth. Place the mixture into a bowl. Place the bread into the food processor and blitz to make breadcrumbs. Add the crumbs to the bowl along with the egg, herbs, lemon juice, vegetable stock and onion mixture. Season well with salt and pepper and stir to combine thoroughly.

Heat the vegetable oil in the frying pan and cook the mushrooms until they are lightly coloured then set aside to cool.

Place one third of the chick pea mixture in the base of the oiled loaf tin, then a layer of cooked mushrooms, then smooth over the second layer of chick pea mixture. Spoon over the last of the mushrooms, finally topping with last third of the chick pea mixture.

Cover with foil and bake for about 45–50 minutes.

Allow to cool in the tin then turn out and wrap in foil or clingfilm. Chill.

If you prefer to slice the bake before you head out, carefully unwrap it, slice it and reassemble into the loaf shape then wrap it back up to transport.

Serve sliced, with green salad, crusty bread and garlic mayonnaise.

No outdoor cookery book could be without a wrap or two. They are very popular these days – so here's my very favourite veggie wrap, packed full of flavour.

Roasted Vegetable, Mozzarella and Hummus Wraps

SERVES 4 • PREPARATION TIME 15 MINUTES • COOKING TIME 50 MINUTES

1 large red onion, *roughly chopped*

1 yellow or orange pepper, *deseeded and cut into 2–3cm chunks*

1 red pepper, *deseeded and cut into 2–3cm chunks*

1 aubergine, *cut into 2–3cm chunks*

2 medium courgettes, *cut into 2–3cm chunks*

2 garlic cloves, *unpeeled and left whole*

sprig of fresh thyme or ½ tsp dried thyme

3 tbsp olive oil

6 sun-dried tomatoes, *chopped*

4 large flour tortillas or multi-seed wraps

200g hummus

150g mozzarella cheese, *sliced*

large handful of torn fresh basil leaves

salt and freshly ground black pepper

Preheat the oven to 190°C/Gas Mark 5.

Spread out all the fresh vegetables on a large baking tray. Add the garlic and thyme, drizzle with the olive oil and turn the vegetables to coat them. Roast in the oven for about 50 minutes, stirring halfway through, until they are beginning to colour and are quite dry.

Remove the tray from the oven, add the sun-dried tomatoes and season with salt and pepper. When cool, squeeze the roasted garlic from its skin, chop and mix back into the roasted vegetables.

Put each wrap on a flat surface. Spread one half of each wrap with one quarter of the hummus, not quite to the edge. Place some one quarter of the roasted vegetables on top, followed one quarter of the mozzarella cheese. Position one quarter of the basil leaves in a line across the centre to the edge of each wrap.

Fold up the side of the wrap where the filling is, fold in the sides and roll up tightly. Slice in half on the diagonal, wrap in foil or clingfilm and chill well.

This is great portable food – easy to make and it cuts well once chilled. I've used ham here but any meat, fish or chopped sausages could be used – it's good with leftover roast beef or lamb too.

Pesto, Potato and Onion Tortilla

SERVES 4 • PREPARATION TIME 15 MINUTES • COOKING TIME 40 MINUTES

3 large potatoes, skin on
4 tbsp oil
2 onions, *finely chopped*
6 medium eggs
190g jar red or green pesto
200g wafer-thin ham

Preheat the oven to 190°C/gas mark 5.

Place the whole potatoes in a pan of boiling water and boil them until cooked through – about 15–20 minutes. Drain the potatoes and remove their skins.

Meanwhile, heat 2 tablespoons of the oil in a large, ovenproof frying pan and cook the onions for 10 minutes to soften. Remove from the pan.

Place the eggs in a jug, add the pesto and mix well with a fork to combine.

Slice the potatoes thickly, then lay half of them in the bottom of the ovenproof frying pan. Drizzle the remaining oil over. Spread the cooked onions evenly over the potatoes and top with half the ham. Pour over half the egg mixture.

Add the remaining potato slices and ham, then finally pour over the rest of the egg mixture.

Bake the tortilla for 20 minutes, or until set firmly. Remove from the oven and set aside to cool, then chill really well.

When you are ready to pack your picnic, remove from the pan, cut the tortilla into wedges and wrap it in clingfilm.

This can be made well in advance and is far better than many of the shop-bought salad dishes you can buy – and certainly cheaper!

I like to use gemelli pasta shapes for this dish, they made from strands of pasta and twisted into a spiral. If you can't get hold of them, any smallish pasta shape is fine.

Roasted Aubergine Salad with Pasta and Fresh Basil

SERVES 2–4 • PREPARATION TIME 10 MINUTES • COOKING TIME 45 MINUTES

1 large aubergine, *cut into 3cm cubes*

1 garlic clove, *unpeeled and left whole*

3 tbsp olive oil

1 tbsp vegetable oil

1 red onion, *sliced*

1 yellow pepper, *deseeded and roughly diced*

50g chorizo, *chopped*

400g can chopped tomatoes

10 large fresh basil leaves, *snipped*

½–1 tsp dried chilli flakes

1 tsp soft brown sugar

175g dried gemelli pasta

25g pecorino cheese, *finely diced*

freshly ground black pepper

Preheat the oven to 190°C/gas mark 5.

Spread the aubergine pieces on to a large oven tray. Add the whole unpeeled garlic clove and drizzle over the olive oil. Roast for about 40 minutes, stirring halfway through, until the aubergine is just beginning to colour.

Remove the tray from the oven. When cool, squeeze the roasted garlic from its skin and stir it into the roasted aubergine.

Meanwhile, heat the vegetable oil in a pan and sauté the onion with the pepper and the chorizo for about 5 minutes.

Stir in the tomatoes, half the basil leaves, the chilli flakes and sugar. Season well with black pepper (no salt – it will be salty enough) cover and leave to simmer for about 15–20 minutes. Add the roasted aubergines to the sauce for the last 5 minutes.

While the sauce is cooking, cook the pasta according to the pack instructions and drain. Add the cooked pasta to the sauce and stir in the remaining basil leaves and diced cheese. Serve at room temperature.

Green Tomato, Potato and Red Onion Pie

SERVES 6–8 • PREPARATION TIME 30 MINUTES • COOKING TIME 50 MINUTES

My grandmother used to make a potato pie with just onions, potatoes and butter – it was truly delicious. Here I have added green (under-ripe) tomatoes as well – great not only for using up any of your home-grown tomatoes that stay stubbornly green but also for adding a distinctive tang.

If you are pressed for time (or simply don't feel in the mood) use 225g ready-made shortcrust pastry instead of making your own.

I like to serve this with Chow Chow, see page 192.

225g plain flour

55g unsalted butter

55g lard

1 medium egg

2 tbsp olive oil

1 red onion, *thinly sliced*

2 tbsp chopped fresh tarragon

500g green tomatoes, *cut into 1cm slices*

2 tsp caster sugar

500g potatoes, *cut into 1cm thick slices*

70g unsalted butter, *melted*

1 medium egg, *lightly beaten*

salt and freshly ground black pepper

The first job is to make the pastry (or not as the case may be!).

Pop the flour, butter, lard and a pinch of salt into a food processor and whizz together until you have fine breadcrumbs. Then add the whole egg and a touch of cold water and mix the whole lot together, but do not overwork.

Preheat the oven to 180°C/gas mark 4.

Turn out the pastry and form it into a flat ball. Cut away about one third and reserve this for the lid.

Roll out the larger quantity of dough and use it to line a 23cm round, 3cm deep loose-based flan tin, making sure you leave enough of the pastry overlapping to stick the lid on to. Chill well.

Next, heat the olive oil in a small pan and gently fry the onion and tarragon together to soften the onion slightly. Spread the cooked onions evenly over the bottom of the pastry base and season well with salt and pepper.

Next, lay on the sliced green tomatoes, and sprinkle over the caster sugar, again, season well with salt and pepper. Top with the sliced potatoes in a circular fashion and yes, a little more salt and pepper! You need to slightly over season this dish so don't be shy! Finally, pour over the melted butter.

Roll out the piece of reserved pastry about 3–4cm larger than the base. Brush the top edge of the flan carefully with the beaten egg. Lay the pastry lid over the potatoes and seal well. Glaze the top of the pie with beaten egg and make a small incision in the middle. Place the pie on a baking tray and pop it into the oven for about 45–50 minutes.

Remove from the oven and leave to cool completely. I think it's best to leave the pie overnight at room temperature, or you can chill it and bring it out of the fridge about an hour before you want to eat.

Bean Dip with Olive Oil and Seed Crackers

Bean Dip with Olive Oil • SERVES 4 • PREPARATION TIME 5 MINUTES

Seed Crackers • MAKES 16–20 CRACKERS • PREPARATION TIME 10 MINUTES PLUS CHILLING • COOKING TIME 20–25 MINUTES

I love beans of any description. Here they form the basis of a chunky dip which makes great snack food. The crackers are fun and easy to make – and I have to say I do prefer them to shop-bought savoury biscuits.

For the bean dip

400g can kidney beans, *drained*

zest of 1 lemon

3 tbsp lemon juice

6 tbsp extra virgin olive oil

400g can chick peas, *drained*

2 tbsp tomato purée

2 tbsp grated Parmesan cheese

1 tsp dried oregano

½ tsp ground cumin

salt and freshly ground black pepper

best-quality extra virgin olive oil and paprika, to serve

For the seed crackers

250g plain flour

1 tsp baking powder

¼ tsp salt

2 tbsp poppy seeds

2 tbsp sesame seeds

2 tsp caraway seeds

60g chilled unsalted butter, *cubed*

freshly ground black pepper

To make the crackers, sift the flour, baking powder, and salt into a medium bowl. Stir in the seeds and some freshly ground black pepper. Rub in the butter until it resembles fine breadcrumbs.

Make a well in the centre of the mixture and add 100ml cold water and mix to a firm dough. Add more water if necessary. Knead the dough into a rough ball but don't knead it too much.

Roll the dough out between two sheets of clingfilm until it is quite thin – it should be about 2mm thick. Remove the top sheet of clingfilm, prick the sheet of dough all over with a fork, then re-cover with the top layer of clingfilm and leave to rest in the fridge for 20 minutes.

Line a baking tray with greaseproof paper. Preheat the oven to 180°C/gas mark 4.

Remove the top layer of clingfilm and cut out 6cm rounds from the dough. Place the rounds on to the lined baking sheet and then bake until lightly golden – 20–25 minutes.

Transfer to a wire cooling rack and leave to cool. Once cold, the crackers will keep for a few days in an airtight container.

To make the dip, place the kidney beans, lemon zest and juice and oil in a food processor and blend to a rough paste. Add the remaining ingredients to the processor and pulse just a few times, to combine together. Transfer to an airtight lidded container.

To serve, drizzle some best-quality olive oil over the top of the dip. Dust with paprika and serve at room temperature with the Seed Crackers.

Grains are a great vehicle to carry different flavours and textures and are very versatile. I sometimes use Israeli couscous, also known as jumbo couscous, in this recipe. Quinoa which has a slightly chewier texture, also works well here. Or alternatively try ebly, a grain made from durum wheat.

Simple Grain Salad with Dried Meats, Fruit and Pine Nuts

SERVES 4 • PREPARATION TIME 10 MINUTES • COOKING TIME 10–15 MINUTES, DEPENDING ON TYPE OF GRAIN USED

200g couscous, Israeli couscous,
    quinoa or Ebly
juice of 1 lime
4 tbsp olive oil
4 spring onions, *sliced on the diagonal*
1 small red pepper, *deseeded and diced*
1 tbsp cooked peas
4 tbsp pine nuts
50g dried cherries, cranberries
    or sultanas
100g cooked dried meats, e.g. salami,
    air-dried ham or cooked sausage,
    thinly sliced
small bunch of fresh parsley or
    coriander, *chopped*
salt and freshly ground black pepper

Cook the grain according to the instructions on the pack; drain well. While still hot, stir in the lime juice and oil and season well. Cool and chill.

When cold, stir in all the other ingredients and pack into an airtight lidded container. Keep chilled until ready to go.

Tasty Turkey Tortilla Bake

PREPARATION TIME 15 MINUTES • COOKING TIME 20 MINUTES • SERVES 4–6

My kids love this – it's good picnic food and it travels well. I like to serve this with a simple salad dressed with lemon and olive oil.

For the bake

2 tbsp olive oil

1 small onion, *finely chopped*

200g mushrooms, *finely sliced*

500g minced turkey

250g frozen peas, *cooked and well drained*

850ml skimmed milk

1 chicken stock cube

70g plain flour

70g unsalted butter, *softened*

2 tsp wholegrain mustard, optional

150g tortilla chips

100g Cheddar cheese, *grated*

For the salad

4 little gem lettuce, *finely sliced*

¼ cucumber, *finely sliced*

juice of ½ lemon

2 tbsp olive oil

Heat the olive oil in a frying pan, then add the onion and mushrooms and cook for a few minutes until slightly browned (this will happen once the moisture from the mushrooms has evaporated).

Add the mince and break it down with a wooden spoon; this may take a couple of minutes. Cook until all the liquid has evaporated, then add the cooked peas.

Meanwhile heat the milk and the stock cube in a separate pan.

Place the flour and butter together into a bowl and mix to a paste. Once the milk is boiling, add the flour and butter paste and whisk well to thicken the sauce nicely.

Add the hot sauce to the cooked turkey mixture, and then add the wholegrain mustard, if using.

Preheat the grill to high.

Spoon half the sauce into a 22 x 32 x 7cm deep baking dish, sprinkle over the tortilla chips, then top evenly with the rest of the sauce. Sprinkle over the cheese, then brown under the grill.

Cool, cut up and wrap in clingfilm. Chill well before packing for the picnic.

For the salad, place the lettuce and cucumber into an airtight lidded bowl, then add the lemon and oil and really mix well.

Serve wedges of the chilled bake with salad on the side.

Meat Loaf

SERVES 6–8 • **PREPARATION TIME** 20 MINUTES • **COOKING TIME** 40–50 MINUTES

I like meat loaf, even though I seem to remember at school it wasn't particularly nice! It has had its fair share of bad publicity over the years, but if made correctly and seasoned well it really is rather good – I had a quite delicious one in America recently. This version is best made a day in advance to allow the flavours to develop.

You can add whole hard-boiled eggs to the meat loaf before you cook it, for a twist on gala pie, if you fancy.

1 tbsp vegetable oil

2 onions, *finely chopped*

500g minced beef, lamb or turkey

200g good-quality sausage meat

1 tsp dried oregano

1 tsp ground cinnamon

1 tsp dried chilli flakes

3 slices white bread, *crusts removed, made into breadcrumbs*

1 medium egg, *beaten*

4 tbsp roughly chopped fresh parsley

3 hard-boiled eggs, *shelled, optional*

vegetable oil, for greasing

salt and freshly ground black pepper

Preheat the oven to 180°C/gas mark 4.

Heat the oil in a small frying pan and add the onions. Cook for 10 minutes to soften slightly, and take a little colour.

Meanwhile, place the meats in a large bowl. Add the oregano, cinnamon, chilli flakes, breadcrumbs, beaten egg and parsley. Season with pepper and just a little salt (sausage meat can be salty) and mix really well.

Once the onions are ready, add them to the meat mixture and mix really well again.

Spoon the mixture into a 450g non-stick loaf tin. If you are adding hard-boiled eggs, place half the meat mixture in the tin, lay the eggs lengthways across the centre of the tin and cover them completely with the remaining meat. Cover the tin tightly with 2 layers of oiled foil.

Place the tin on a baking tray (to catch any fat that may come out) and pop into the oven. Cook for 40–50 minutes, or until the juices run clear once a knife is inserted. Once cooked, carefully remove from the oven and set aside to cool in the tin.

Once cool, press lightly on the foil, then place a thick piece of cardboard or thin piece of wood on top of the foil and balance a couple of cans of beans or tomatoes on top (this makes it easier to slice once cooled). Pop into the fridge and chill well – overnight is best.

Once chilled, remove from the tin and slice, and wrap in foil or clingfilm, ready for the picnic.

This sort of sandwich, with a thin escalope of meat that is floured, dipped in egg and breadcrumbs before frying, is all the rage in Europe. I think it's a nice way to enjoy cuts of meat that are difficult to cook due to the fact they dry out quickly because they have little or no fat at all.

I like to serve venison schnitzel but pork fillet, lamb loins and pheasant and chicken breasts, will all work successfully when cooked in this way.

Venison Pesto Schnitzel Sandwiches

SERVES 4 • PREPARATION TIME 20 MINUTES • COOKING TIME 6–8 MINUTES

For the sandwiches

4 x 150g slices venison

3 tbsp plain flour

2 medium eggs, *beaten*

8 tbsp dried breadcrumbs

50g unsalted butter

50ml olive oil

4 individual ciabattas, *halved lengthways*

4 tbsp red pesto

For the dressing

1 small red onion, *very finely chopped*

3 tbsp red wine vinegar

2 pinches of caster sugar

6 tbsp extra virgin olive oil

6 tbsp chopped fresh parsley

salt and freshly ground black pepper

Place each piece of venison between 2 pieces of lightly wetted clingfilm and gently flatten it with a rolling pin or meat mallet, the thinner the better. Place the flour, beaten eggs and dried breadcrumbs into 3 separate wide, shallow bowls. Dip each flattened slice of meat into the flour, then the beaten egg and breadcrumbs, pressing the crumbs down well.

Meanwhile, place all the ingredients for the dressing into a bowl, season well and stir well to combine.

Heat the butter and oil in a large frying pan until it is foaming. Add the schnitzels and cook for 3–4 minutes on each side until nicely browned, then set aside to cool.

Open the ciabatta and spread the 8 halves with red pesto. Add the cooled schnitzels and a good spoonful of the dressing. Place the top on each sandwich and wrap them well in foil. Chill until you are ready to go on the picnic.

This is my take on the classic US sandwich. I call this a hefty sandwich, because that's exactly what it is, but great for filling you up on a trip or long walk – or maybe just for a lunchtime treat at your desk?

New York Deli Sandwich

SERVES 2 • PREPARATION TIME 10 MINUTES

For the horseradish mayo
3 tbsp mayonnaise
2 tsp horseradish sauce
dash of Worcestershire Sauce

For the sandwich
20g unsalted butter
4 slices of rye bread
200g salt beef or pastrami
2 tbsp sauerkraut, *well drained*
handful of watercress or
   spinach leaves
freshly ground black pepper

Mix the mayonnaise with the horseradish and the Worcestershire Sauce. (You can substitute mild mustard for the horseradish if you prefer.)

Spread the butter on the bread.

For each sandwich, spread half the mayonnaise over one slice of bread and season with black pepper. Arrange half the salt beef on top of the mayonnaise and then top with half the sauerkraut. Spread the watercress or spinach over the whole slice and cover with the second slice of bread.

Press the sandwich gently together, slice and wrap in foil or clingfilm.

These are delicious hot or cold. Gently cook them so they are just warmed through and eat straightaway, or leave to chill in the fridge ready to take on a picnic. You can also cook these on the barbecue if you like.

Bitter Chocolate and Banana Caramel Fudge Wraps

SERVES 4 • PREPARATION TIME 10 MINUTES • COOKING TIME 4–6 MINUTES

4 bananas
100g plain chocolate, *roughly chopped*
4 tbsp ready-made caramel toffee
   (available in cans or jars)
finely grated zest of 1 large lime
squeeze of lime juice
4 soft flour tortillas
1 medium egg white, *lightly beaten*

Light a charcoal barbecue and wait until the coals are grey or preheat a gas barbecue to medium.

Chop the bananas into small pieces and place in a medium bowl. Add the chopped chocolate, caramel toffee, lime zest and juice and stir well.

Brush each wrap with a little beaten egg white. Place a quarter of the filling on each wrap, tuck in the ends and roll up. Place on a baking tray and cook on the hot barbecue until crisp and slightly coloured, probably 2–3 minutes each side. Do not overcook the wraps – the chocolate should not be completely melted.

Leave the wraps to cool, then chill in the fridge. Once chilled they are ready for the picnic hamper.

This really chewy muesli bar is packed full of flavour and energy. Great for taking on long walks or lazy picnics – depending on what kind of a mood you're in!

They are best made at least a day in advance to allow their deliciously moist and chewy texture to develop.

Fruit and Nut Muesli Bars

MAKES 12 BARS • PREPARATION TIME 10 MINUTES • COOKING TIME 20 MINUTES

200g unsalted butter

80g golden syrup

75g soft brown sugar

40g clear honey

300g rolled porridge oats

50g mixed dried berry fruits

40g dried apricots, *chopped*

25g hazelnuts, with skin,
    roughly chopped

25g pecan nuts, *roughly chopped*

75g mixed seeds, e.g. sunflower,
    pumpkin, linseed, hemp, sesame

Preheat the oven to 180°C/gas mark 4. Line a 28 x 20 x 4cm non-stick baking tin with baking parchment.

Place the butter, syrup, sugar and honey in a medium pan and heat gently, stirring until the butter has melted and the sugar dissolved.

Remove from the heat and stir in the oats, fruits, nuts and seeds.

Press the mixture lightly into the lined tray. Bake for about 20 minutes until light golden brown.

Allow to cool in the tin for 5 minutes and then score lightly with a knife into 12 bars. Leave until completely cold and wrap in foil or clingfilm.

These will keep in an airtight container for up to 4 days.

On the following few pages is a selection of my favourite baked loaves. These are, in effect, giant sandwiches – ideal for slicing and sharing – and perfect for picnics.

Sun-blush Tomato, Hummus and Roasted Pepper Baked Loaf

SERVES 6–8 • PREPARATION TIME 20 MINUTES • COOKING TIME 30–40 MINUTES

1 large cottage loaf
4–6 tbsp olive oil
100g sun-blush tomatoes
1 bunch fresh coriander, *finely chopped*
200g smoked tofu, *sliced thinly*
100g hummus
90g jar red pesto
100g roasted red and yellow peppers, from a jar

Preheat the oven to 200°C/gas mark 6.

Cut the loaf horizontally into 5 slices. Lay each slice on to a chopping board. Spoon the olive oil evenly over the sliced bread, then season each slice with salt and pepper.

On the large base slice of bread, lay the sun-blush tomatoes, then arrange the chopped coriander evenly over the top.

Lay the next slice of bread on top, and arrange the smoked tofu on it. Then lay another slice of bread over top and spread on the hummus evenly. Top again with another slice of bread, spread over the red pesto, and arrange the peppers on top. Lastly, place the final crust back in position.

Place the loaf on to a very large piece of foil and completely wrap it up. Wrap it in a second large piece of foil and squeeze nice and tightly. Place on a baking tray and pop into the oven for 30–40 minutes.

Once cooked remove from the oven and press nice and tightly again, be quite brutal here, the more you press the better the chilled loaf will cut the next day. Cool and chill well, overnight is best if possible.

Next day, remove from the fridge and take on your picnic. Slice to serve.

Another picnic favourite in the Vickery household – my kids came up with the idea of mixing and matching the fillings and this is the rather unusual, but really tasty result.

Kids' All-in-one Baked Sandwich Loaf

SERVES 6–8 • **PREPARATION TIME** 20 MINUTES • **COOKING TIME** 30–40 MINUTES

1 large cottage loaf
4–6 tbsp olive oil
200g shaved turkey or ham
210g can sweetcorn, *drained*
6 smoked sausages, *sliced lengthways*
200g Edam cheese, *very thinly sliced*
200g can baked beans
salt and freshly ground black pepper

Preheat the oven to 200°C/gas mark 6.

Cut the loaf horizontally into 5 slices. Lay each slice on to a chopping board. Spoon the olive oil evenly over the sliced bread, then season each slice with salt and pepper.

On the base slice of bread, evenly arrange the turkey or ham and sweetcorn. Place the next slice of bread on top, and then lay over the smoked sausages.

Lay the next slice of bread on top and evenly spread over the Edam cheese. Top with the next slice of bread and finally spoon over the baked beans. Replace the final crust on the top.

Place the loaf on to a very large piece of foil and completely wrap it up. Wrap it in a second large piece of foil and squeeze nice and tightly. Place on a baking tray and pop into the oven for 30–40 minutes.

Once cooked remove from the oven and press nice and tightly again, be quite brutal here, the more you press the better the chilled loaf will cut the next day. Cool and chill well, best overnight.

Next day, remove from the fridge and take on your picnic. Open and slice to order.

Here's a fish version of the picnic loaf - you could of course use any type of fish, but I quite like the balance between smoked fish, shellfish and marinated fish. I use marinated anchovies rather than the salted variety.

Smoked Salmon, Prawn and Crab Baked Loaf

SERVES 6–8 • PREPARATION TIME 20 MINUTES • COOKING TIME 30–40 MINUTES

1 large cottage loaf
4–6 tbsp olive oil
100g brown crab meat
100g marinated anchovies
100g prawns
100g smoked salmon slices
100g white crab meat
50g rocket
salt and freshly ground black pepper

Preheat the oven to 200°C/gas mark 6.

Cut the loaf horizontally into 5 slices. Lay each slice on to a chopping board. Spoon the olive oil evenly over the sliced bread, then season each slice with salt and pepper.

On the large base slice of bread, evenly spread the brown crabmeat over. Lay the next slice of bread on top, and then arrange the anchovies over.

Lay the next slice of bread on top and arrange the prawns and the smoked salmon on it. Top with the next slice of bread and place the white crab meat and the rocket on it. Top with the final crust.

Place the loaf on to a very large piece of foil and completely wrap it up. Wrap it in a second large piece of foil and squeeze nice and tightly. Place on a baking tray and pop into the oven for 30–40 minutes.

Once cooked remove from the oven and press nice and tightly again. Be quite brutal here – the more you press, the better the chilled loaf will cut the next day. Cool and chill well, overnight is best, if possible.

Next day, when you're ready to go out, remove it from the fridge and open and slice to order, it really is that simple!

This is probably my favourite picnic loaf. The combination may sound a bit odd but it really does work well and the mayonnaise helps to bring everything together.

Leftover Baked Picnic Loaf

SERVES 6–8 • **PREPARATION TIME** 20 MINUTES • **COOKING TIME** 30–40 MINUTES

1 large cottage loaf
4–6 tbsp olive oil
6 slices crispy streaky bacon, *cooked*
2 hard-boiled eggs, *sliced*
6 tbsp garlic mayonnaise
350g can corned beef, *cut into 5 slices*
2 beef tomatoes, each sliced into 4
150g pickled beetroot, *sliced*
salt and freshly ground black pepper

Preheat the oven to 200°C/gas mark 6.

Cut the loaf horizontally into 5 slices. Lay each slice on to a chopping board. Spoon the olive oil evenly over the sliced bread, then season each slice with salt and pepper.

On the large base slice of bread, lay the crispy bacon, sliced boiled eggs and half the mayonnaise. Lay the next slice of bread on top, and then lay over the sliced corned beef.

Lay the next slice of bread on top and spread over the sliced tomato and the remaining mayo. Top with the next slice of bread and arrange the beetroot evenly over. Top with the final crust.

Place the loaf on to a very large piece of foil and completely wrap it up. Wrap it in a second large piece of foil and squeeze nice and tightly. Place on a baking tray and pop into the oven for 30–40 minutes.

Once cooked remove from the oven and press nice and tightly again, be quite brutal here, the more you press the better the chilled loaf will cut the next day. Cool and chill well, best overnight.

Next day, remove from the fridge and take on your picnic. Open and slice to serve.

Baked pudding brioche is easy to transport and makes an unusual, but yummy, end to a picnic. It's quite nice to have a balance of fruit and sweetness, so any fruit will do, but I would steer clear of any that is too juicy such as oranges. If you can leave the brioche out, unwrapped, for a day or two before you make this, all the better.

All-in-one Baked Pudding Brioche

SERVES 6–8 • **PREPARATION TIME** 15 MINUTES • **COOKING TIME** 20 MINUTES

1 large slightly stale brioche loaf

200g clotted cream

4 tbsp ready-made caramel toffee
   (available in cans or jars)

200g strawberries, *halved*

4 tbsp brown sugar

150g white chocolate, *finely chopped*

3 medium bananas, *sliced*

clotted cream, to serve

Preheat the oven to 200°C/gas mark 6.

Cut the brioche horizontally into 5 even slices. Spread the clotted cream and caramel evenly over 4 brioche slices, leaving the top crust plain.

Layer all 4 slices with strawberries, sugar, chocolate and banana. Stack the slices back together and place the crust on top. Wrap tightly in foil and bake for 20 minutes.

Once cooked remove the loaf from the oven and make sure it is still tightly wrapped, cool and chill well, preferably overnight.

Next day, remove from the fridge and take on your picnic. Serve sliced with perhaps a little more clotted cream.

Chapter 7
FROM THE FLASK

As a young child growing up, a hot or cold flask of drink or food always seemed to feature in family life. My father would take a flask to work with him, and we would always have a flask of tea when we went for a Sunday walk, especially in the colder months. When my brothers and I were learning to swim, my parents would take us to an open-air swimming pool in the summer. The water was so cold that I can remember not being able to stop shivering for hours afterwards. However, my dad would always make a flask of hot Bovril to revive us and to this day I remember that delicious, satisfying warming savoury beef flavour.

With all that in mind, I thought it would be fun to create a range of year-round foods that can be served straight from the flask. Some are hearty and filling and ideal for a cold winter's day, some just simple and refreshing and perfect for a boiling hot summer's day. I have even provided a few cocktails! All of the recipes have gone down really well with my friends and family, so I hope you enjoy them too.

There are many regional variations of this Spanish classic, and this version always works for me. I like to add a little Worcestershire Sauce for extra kick and plenty of olive oil. I also like to use sherry vinegar because I find that it has a soft, sweet flavour, but any will do really. Just remember to chill the soup well before pouring it into the flask.

Chilled Gazpacho

SERVES 4–6 • **PREPARATION TIME** 15 MINUTES PLUS CHILLING

2 red peppers, *deseeded and roughly chopped*

2 yellow peppers, *deseeded and roughly chopped*

½ cucumber, *peeled*

400g can chopped tomatoes

4 garlic cloves, *roughly chopped*

1 onion, *roughly chopped*

1 litre good-quality tomato juice

2 slices white bread, *roughly broken up*

150ml extra virgin olive oil

1 tbsp Worcestershire Sauce

2 tsp Tabasco Sauce

2 tbsp sherry vinegar

1 tbsp sugar

salt and freshly ground black pepper

Place the vegetables, tomato juice, bread and oil in a food processor or blender and process until smooth. Pass the mixture through a fairly fine sieve.

Add the Worcestershire Sauce, Tabasco Sauce, sherry vinegar and sugar, and mix well. Finally season to taste.

Chill well and transfer to a flask. Serve in mugs, cups or glasses.

A lassi is a yogurt-based Indian drink. This version is a perfect for thirst-quenching summer drink.

Melon and Cucumber Lassi

SERVES 4 • **PREPARATION TIME** 10 MINUTES

1 small honeydew, galia or cantaloupe
   ripe melon
1 cucumber, *peeled and chopped*
juice of 2 limes
6 fresh basil leaves
4 tbsp Greek yogurt
1–2 tablespoons clear honey
good handful of ice cubes

Cut the melon in half and scoop out the seeds. Using a spoon, scoop the flesh into a food processor or blender. Add the chopped cucumber and lime juice and blitz well.

Add the basil to the food processor with the yogurt, 1 tbsp of the honey and the ice cubes.

Blend until smooth, then taste and add more honey if you think it needs it. Transfer to a flask and serve in glasses or cups.

Any summer produce will work well in this refreshing vegetable soup, which can be served hot or chilled. The delicate flavour of the lemon verbena adds a distinctive citrus tang. Don't worry if you can't get hold of it – you can use lemon balm, or failing that the finely grated zest of 1 large lemon will add a great flavour too.

Summer Vegetable Soup with Lemon Verbena

SERVES 4 • **PREPARATION TIME** 15 MINUTES PLUS CHILLING IF SERVING COLD • **COOKING TIME** 25–30 MINUTES

4 tbsp olive oil

¼ tsp chilli powder

½ tsp ground cumin

1 tsp ground turmeric

2 tbsp kalonji seeds

1 small onion, *finely chopped*

3 garlic cloves, *roughly chopped*

1 carrot, *roughly chopped*

1 courgette, *roughly chopped*

1 small aubergine, *roughly chopped*

2 vegetable stock cubes

400g can cannellini beans, *drained*

4 handfuls baby spinach leaves

100g frozen peas

100g mangetout, *roughly chopped*

4 tbsp chopped fresh coriander

4 tbsp chopped fresh lemon verbena
    (or lemon balm, or finely grated
    zest of 1 large lemon)

salt and freshly ground black pepper

Heat the oil in a large saucepan, add the spices and cook for 2–3 minutes.

Add the onion, garlic, carrot, courgette, aubergine, 1 litre boiling water and stock cubes and bring to the boil. Cook for 20 minutes until the vegetables are cooked.

Add the beans, spinach, peas, mange tout and coriander and cook for a further 5 minutes.

Season well with salt and pepper, then add the lemon verbena, lemon balm, or lemon zest.

If serving hot, transfer to a flask straight away. Alternatively allow the soup to cool and then chill well.

This simple soup is packed with flavour, is really good for you and makes a lovely light starter or main course. I like to use sachets of good-quality instant miso soup (available from major supermarkets) as they make a great base for a stock or soup.

The broth can be served hot or cold – just remember to allow enough time to chill it thoroughly if you are planning to eat it chilled.

Iceberg Lettuce, Smoked Tofu and Pea Broth

SERVES 4 • PREPARATION TIME 10 MINUTES PLUS CHILLING IF SERVING COLD • COOKING TIME 20 MINUTES

560ml boiling water

1 vegetable stock cube

2 x 15g sachets instant miso soup

1 large onion, *finely chopped*

2 garlic cloves, *crushed*

½ head of iceberg lettuce, *finely chopped or sliced*

150g frozen peas

200g smoked tofu, *cut into ½-cm cubes*

salt and freshly ground black pepper

Place the water, stock cube, miso, onion and garlic into a saucepan and bring to the boil. Turn the heat down and simmer for 10 minutes, or until the onion has softened.

Add the lettuce, peas and tofu and simmer for 10 minutes.

Season well and if serving hot, transfer to a flask straight away. Alternatively allow the broth to cool and then chill well.

I used to make this as a lightly jellied summer starter in the restaurant. One day a chef forgot to add the gelatine and left it to chill in the fridge. I decided to serve it as chilled soup so as not to waste it and it was a roaring success!

Chilled Salmon, Saffron and Tomato Soup with Tarragon

SERVES 2 • PREPARATION TIME 15 MINUTES PLUS CHILLING • COOKING TIME 20 MINUTES

1 tbsp olive oil

1 medium onion, *finely chopped*

1 garlic clove, *chopped*

1 tbsp sherry vinegar

1 tsp soft brown sugar

a few saffron strands

100ml vermouth or white wine

150ml vegetable stock

400g passata

200g salmon fillet, *skinned and cut into 1cm cubes*

75g baby plum or cherry tomatoes, *finely diced*

1 tbsp snipped fresh tarragon leaves

salt and freshly ground black pepper

Heat the oil in a medium pan and add the onion and garlic. Cook for 5 minutes to soften slightly.

Stir in the vinegar, sugar, saffron and vermouth and let it bubble for a couple of minutes. Add the stock and passata and bring back to a simmer. Season well and cook gently, uncovered, for 10–15 minutes until reduced a little.

Set the tomato soup aside to cool and then chill it thoroughly.

Bring a pan of water to simmering point and poach the salmon very briefly until very lightly cooked – this will take about 1 minute. Drain and chill.

Stir the chilled salmon into the soup and transfer it to the flask.

Pack the chopped tomatoes and tarragon separately, to add to the soup when serving from the flask.

This simple refreshing summer cooler is a great alternative to fizzy drinks for the kids (and adults too, of course!) and they'll enjoy helping to make it too.

If you have enough time, freeze the mango cubes in advance for a really cool drink!

Iced Mango and Forest Fruit Crush

SERVES 2 • PREPARATION TIME 10 MINUTES

2 mangoes, *flesh cubed* (or 255g
   drained weight canned mangoes)
200g frozen red berries or fruits of the
   forest mix
50ml apple juice
zest and juice of 1 lime

Put the mango cubes, frozen berries and apple juice into a blender or food processor and pulse briefly until you have a chunky mixture. Add the lime zest and juice, stir through and fill the flask straight away to keep the mixture slushy.

This is summer drinking at its best – sure to make your picnic go with a swing! Serve these fruity cocktails as cold as possible, so to chill the flask before you add the drink, add a few ice cubes to the flask, give it a shake then discard the ice.

If you're a fan of cooling summer cocktails, it's a good idea to have some sugar syrup ready in the fridge (see below) as it can be used for the basis of lots of marvellous concoctions!

Tequila and Lime Iced Fruit Cocktails

SERVES 2 • PREPARATION TIME 10 MINUTES

100g unrefined cane sugar

juice of 1 lime (about 45ml)

juice of 1 pink grapefruit (about 150ml) plus the pulp and juicy bits

60ml Tequila

ice, to top up the flask

To make the sugar syrup, place the sugar and 100ml water in a small pan. Bring to a gentle boil, then reduce the heat and simmer until the sugar is completely dissolved and the syrup is slightly thickened – this will take about 3 minutes. Leave to cool and then chill in the fridge.

Place the lime juice, grapefruit juice (with pulp and juicy bits), Tequila and 100ml sugar syrup into a chilled 500ml flask. Add enough ice cubes to fill the flask and seal. The ice will dilute the drink when melted, so there is no need to add any water.

Pomegranate and Passionfruit Kick

SERVES 2 • PREPARATION TIME 10 MINUTES

juice of 1 lime (about 45ml)

60ml Tequila

30ml sugar syrup, chilled, see above

100ml pomegranate juice drink

200ml passionfruit juice drink

ice cubes, to serve

Combine all the ingredients into a chilled 500ml flask. If you can, take another flask to store some ice cubes for adding to the drinks as you pour them.

This is a lovely, light and creamy soup, packed full of flavour. Just right for lunch halfway through a walk on a spring or autumn day – take along some wholemeal bread spread thickly with butter to help keep you going.

Prawn, Potato and Onion Chowder

SERVES 4 • **PREPARATION TIME** 15 MINUTES • **COOKING TIME** 30 MINUTES

16 raw freshwater prawns

25g unsalted butter

1 medium onion, *finely chopped*

350g waxy potatoes, *cut into 2cm cubes*

1 medium carrot, *cut into 1cm cubes*

1 medium stick celery, *sliced*

300ml fish or vegetable stock

170g can evaporated milk

1 bay leaf

¼ tsp celery salt

¼ tsp mustard powder

3 cardamom pods, *crushed and seeds removed*

2 tbsp roughly chopped fresh parsley

freshly ground black pepper

wholemeal bread and butter, *to serve*

To prepare the prawns, break off the heads and peel off the shells (these can be reserved to make fish stock for another time). Run a small sharp knife down the back of each prawn and pull out the black thread.

Melt the butter in a large, heavy-based pan over a gentle heat. Add the onion and cook for 5 minutes to soften slightly.

Add the remaining vegetables, stock, evaporated milk, bay leaf, celery salt, mustard powder and cardamom seeds to the pan, season with black pepper and bring to the boil.

Turn the heat down, cover and then simmer gently for about 15 minutes until the vegetables are soft. Take care that the milky stock does not boil up and over during cooking.

Stir in the prawns and cook for another few minutes only, just until the prawns turn pink. Stir the parsley through the soup and then fill the flask with the piping hot soup. Serve with chunks of buttered wholemeal bread.

This soup is a nice way to kick off an outdoor meal, either chilled in the summer, or gently heated through in a pan in the autumn or winter, and then poured into a flask.

Bloody Mary Stew with Black Olives and Celery Salt

SERVES 4 • **PREPARATION TIME** 10 MINUTES

100ml vodka

400g can chopped tomatoes

3 tbsp lemon juice

2 tsp celery salt

4 tsp caster sugar

4 tbsp olive oil

½ tsp chilli powder

1 tbsp Worcestershire Sauce

2 small onions, *finely chopped*

1 garlic clove, *crushed*

100g pitted black olives,
   roughly chopped

6 fresh vine-ripened tomatoes,
   chopped

salt and freshly ground black pepper

olive oil and crusty bread, to serve

This one's so simple – pop everything in a liquidiser or food processor, apart from the olives and the fresh tomatoes, add 200ml water, then blitz for a couple of minutes until smooth.

Taste and check the seasoning, then add the olives and chopped tomatoes. Chill well, if you want to enjoy the soup cold. Pop into the flask and off you go.

Serve with a drizzle of olive oil and chunks of fresh, crusty bread.

When we were kids my dad would take us swimming in an outdoor pool, it was freezing! To warm us up afterwards he would make hot Bovril for us. I have loved it ever since and still enjoy it at football matches.

So, here is a soup based on that unforgettable flavour that brings back so many memories for me.

Corned Beef, Bovril and Potato Hash

SERVES 4 • PREPARATION TIME 10 MINUTES • COOKING TIME 30 MINUTES

3 tbsp vegetable oil

1 large onion, *finely chopped*

400g potatoes, *cut into 3cm dice*

1 tbsp Bovril

400ml boiling water

2–3 tbsp Worcestershire Sauce

340g can corned beef, *chilled, fat removed and cut into 3cm pieces*

3 tbsp roughly chopped fresh parsley

freshly ground black pepper

pickled walnuts or pickled red cabbage, to serve

Heat the oil in a large, heavy-based pan and add the onion. Cook for 5–10 minutes to soften slightly, and take on a little colour.

Add the potatoes and stir. Dissolve the Bovril in the boiling water and add to the pan along with 2 tbsp of the Worcestershire Sauce, season with black pepper. Bring back to the boil, cover the pan and turn the heat down to simmer gently.

Cook for about 20 minutes, or until the potatoes are tender and starting to break up. The potato will thicken the stock; you may need to add a little more water if it is very thick.

Once the potatoes are cooked, add the chunks of corned beef, stir and heat through for a further few minutes only, or it will break up.

Add the roughly chopped parsley and season to taste with black pepper and a little more Worcestershire Sauce. Fill the flask and pack some pickles to eat with the hash.

The original recipe for this seems to have been a basic Bloody Mary,
which was warmed with beef consommé to make it a hot drink. Over
the years it's become a great favourite with the shooting community. It's
always a nice treat on a freezing day – this really is an old-school recipe!

Bullshot

SERVES 2 • **PREPARATION TIME** 5 MINUTES • **COOKING TIME** 5 MINUTES

400ml strong beef stock

a large pinch of celery salt

a dash of Tabasco Sauce

4 dashes of Worcestershire Sauce

1 tbsp lemon or lime juice

50ml vodka

freshly ground black pepper

Heat the beef stock in a small pan. Stir in the celery salt, sauces, lemon or lime juice and season well with black pepper. Heat through until piping hot.

Remove from the heat, stir in the vodka and pour into a flask straight away and seal.

I went shooting many years ago and we were given this soup for lunch. It sounded quite unusual and I never thought it would work, but it certainly does and it's actually rather delicious.

Pigeon and Barley Soup with Allspice, Sage and Onion Stuffing

SERVES 4 • PREPARATION TIME 20 MINUTES • COOKING TIME 1 HOUR

10g dried wild mushrooms

250ml boiling water

25g butter

1 small onion, *finely chopped*

4 skinned and boned pigeon breasts (about 200g total weight), *cut into 5mm cubes*

1 tsp ground allspice

175g swede, *cut into 1–2cm cubes*

300g waxy potatoes, *cut into 1–2cm cubes*

1 small parsnip, *cut into 1–2cm cubes*

1 small carrot, *cut into 1–2cm cubes*

1 small leek, *halved lengthways and thinly sliced*

2 small sticks celery, *finely sliced*

40g pearl barley

600ml vegetable stock

1 bay leaf

1 heaped tsp dried sage

1 thick slice white bread

freshly ground black pepper

Soak the dried mushrooms in the boiling water and set aside.

Heat the butter in a large heavy-based pan over gentle heat and add the onion. Cook for 10 minutes or until it softens slightly and takes on a little colour.

Toss the diced pigeon breast in the allspice. Add the pigeon to the pan with the onions and cook for a couple of minutes, stirring well.

Add the vegetables, the barley, stock and mushrooms with all the soaking liquid. Season well with black pepper, pop the bay leaf in and cover the pan. Simmer on a low heat for about 45 minutes. Check occasionally and top up with a little boiling water if the barley has soaked up all the juices.

Meanwhile whizz the bread in a food processor to make breadcrumbs.

Mix the sage into the breadcrumbs, stir into the thick soup and fill the flask with the hot, chunky mixture.

Chapter 8
FOR THE MORE ADVENTUROUS

In this section are all the oddball foods and cooking methods that didn't fit into the other chapters! There is a mini-section on smoking, something that is very close to my heart. I'm a big fan of the slow smoked foods so beloved in the east coast of America.

Home smoking has really taken off in the past few years, and smoked food is all the rage. These days you can buy many types of smoker from kitchen suppliers or over the internet. They range from small stove-top ones that use a fine sawdust or even wood chips, to more elaborate stand-alone varieties. In this chapter I use a Bradley smoker as they are easy to use, and have a complete cooking range, from cold to hot smoking. The company also sells a range of wood briquettes including apple, hickory and cherry.

In the following pages you will also find some great party pieces including a barbecued Christmas turkey, a whole roast suckling pig and a giant cupcake filled with huge amounts of ice cream.

Soaking a whole turkey in brine may seem like a bit of a faff but it really does improve the flavour and succulence of the meat – try it for Christmas or Thanksgiving. Once you've tasted it you'll realise all that effort was worthwhile! Bear in mind due to the sugar and salt brine the bird will cook darker and brown fairly quickly, so keep an eye on the turkey during the cooking – you may need to cover it with foil at some point to prevent the browning going too far.

You will need a deep plastic or stainless steel bucket deep enough to hold the turkey and all the marinade ingredients. Serve the sliced meat with my Gin and Cranberry Relish – perfect!

Tangerine Brined Whole Turkey

SERVES 8–10 • **PREPARATION TIME** 20 MINUTES PLUS 24 HOURS BRINING AND RESTING TIME • **COOKING TIME** 3 HOURS

For the brine

2 litres apple juice

2 litres dry cider

1kg soft brown sugar

350g sea salt

20 cloves

2 heads garlic, *crushed*

6 tbsp coriander seeds

4 tbsp black peppercorns

4 large sprigs fresh rosemary

12 tangerines or satsumas, *quartered*

For the turkey

5kg turkey

200ml olive oil

200ml boiling water

Gin and Cranberry Relish (page 193),
    to serve

Place all the brine ingredients, apart from the tangerines or satsumas into a stainless steel pan. Squeeze the tangerine or satsuma quarters, by hand, over the pan and add the skins to the pan too. Bring to the boil then simmer for 10 minutes, or until all the sugar and salt has dissolved. Set aside to cool completely.

Transfer the cooled brine to the plastic or stainless steel bucket and place the turkey in, breast side down. Place 3 large plates on top of the turkey to keep it under the brine. Place in the fridge for 24 hours.

Next day, remove the turkey and discard the brine. Rinse the turkey, and pat it dry with kitchen paper, then rub half the olive oil all over the bird. Place it in a roasting tin. Preheat the barbecue; if using gas, the temperature should be set to 200°C.

Pour the boiling water around the turkey, then cover it with foil. Immediately put the turkey on the barbecue and cook for 2 hours.

Remove the foil, rub the remaining oil all over the bird and cook for a further 1 hour, or until it is well browned and cooked through. Remove the bird from the barbecue, tip off the juices and keep for the base of a wonderful gravy. Then return it to the barbecue, put the lid down or cover with foil and leave to rest for 45–60 minutes. Carve and serve with the relish.

Forget the usual Christmas turkey and give this one a go! You will need 6kg charcoal briquettes – 4kg at the start, then a further 2kg at roughly the 3-hour mark. I also use a chimney starter (see page 10), which makes a huge difference to getting the coals started. When it comes to adding more charcoal at the 3-hour point, start the coals in the chimney starter a good 30 minutes beforehand. This will ensure that the temperature stays as constant as possible.

Christmas Turkey on the Barbecue

SERVES 8–10 • **PREPARATION TIME** 20 MINUTES PLUS RESTING TIME • **COOKING TIME** ABOUT 4 HOURS

5–6kg turkey, *wishbone removed (ask your butcher to do this)*

Coriander, Apricot and Fig Stuffing (see page 193) or 750g of your chosen stuffing

2 tbsp vegetable oil

300ml white wine

50ml olive oil

salt and freshly ground black pepper

Preheat a large barbecue with a lid. Remove the turkey from the fridge and leave it for 1 hour to allow it to come to room temperature.

Next light 4kg of charcoal briquettes on the barbecue – I use a chimney starter at this stage. Once hot, place the coals into the barbecue baskets at each end of the barbecue or if your barbecue does not have baskets, then pile them at each end of the barbecue, leaving the centre free.

Stuff the turkey with the stuffing, and tie the legs loosely together with string. Season well all over, then rub with the oil. Combine the white wine and olive oil in a jug. Place the stuffed turkey in a roasting tray, then place the tray in the centre of the barbecue, so it is not directly over the charcoal. Add a couple of glasses of water to the tray, this will prevent the bird from burning and also keeps the air moist whilst it cooks. Top up the water during the cooking time if necessary – there should always be some in the tray. Close and let the temperature cool down slightly.

Cook the turkey for 4 hours, brush with the wine and oil mixture occasionally and check the water levels regularly. You may need to vary the heat of the barbecue by opening and closing the top vent on the kettle, and the vent underneath. The more the vent is open underneath the hotter the charcoal will burn. The more the vent is open on top, the more heat can escape, so cooling down the coals. If both vents are shut, the heat is kept in. It takes a bit of practice, but you will soon get the hang of it.

Once cooked (the internal temperature of the bird should be a minimum of 170°C), remove from the barbecue, cover tightly with foil and leave in a warm place to rest for 45–60 minutes. Serve in the normal way.

This recipe is not for the faint-hearted! It's quite involved but fabulous when cooked – even my youngest daughter loves it. You will need a separate rotisserie attachment for the barbecue.

Hares are relatively simple to get hold of these days from a good butcher. They have quite a strong flavour, and slowly cooked wrapped in bacon they makes a great winter barbecue dish. Yes, I barbecue all year round, even when it snows!

2 hares, about 1.8kg each
20 slices streaky bacon

For the brine
20 cloves
30 juniper berries, *crushed*
1 tbsp caraway seeds
4 tbsp garlic granules
2 tbsp black mustard seeds
3 sprigs fresh rosemary
6 bay leaves
150g sea or rock salt
150g caster sugar
2 tbsp puréed ginger (from a jar)
500ml red wine
100ml red wine vinegar
120g maple syrup
Cumberland Glaze (see page 188)

For the mop
400ml red wine
400ml vegetable oil

Spit-roasted Hare with Smoked Bacon and Cumberland Glaze

SERVES 6–8 • **PREPARATION TIME** 20 MINUTES PLUS AT LEAST 10 HOURS BRINING • **COOKING TIME** 2½–3 HOURS

The day before you want to barbecue the hare, place all the brine ingredients in a stainless steel pan, large enough to put the hares in, and bring to the boil. Simmer for 5 minutes, then cool.

Thoroughly wash the hares inside and out. Place in the cooled brine, put 2 plates on top, then leave in the fridge for at least 10 hours or overnight.

Next day, remove the hares and rinse off the brine and pat dry. Wrap them in the bacon slices, securing with cocktail sticks. Thread the hares carefully on to the rotisserie skewer and secure well. Combine the red wine and vegetable oil for the mop sauce.

Preheat the barbecue to 180°C, using the front or rear burner only, leaving the middle clear. Place the rotisserie skewer on the barbecue, and place a small tray or pan of boiling water next to the rotisserie – this will keep the meat moist and tender. Cook the hares for 2½–3 hours, basting with the mop sauce every 30 minutes. Regularly top up the tray or pan with boiling water from a kettle.

While the hares are cooking make the Cumberland glaze.

Once the hares are cooked they will have taken on a wonderful colour and aroma. Carefully remove them from the rotisserie and place on a baking tray.

Brush half the Cumberland glaze all over the hares, then wrap them in foil and leave for 30 minutes to rest. After resting, you can also pop the unwrapped cooked hares onto a hot barbecue to really caramelise, but take care as they will burn very quickly. Remove the cocktail sticks from the hares and leave the bacon on.

Pull the hare apart and eat it with your fingers dipping, the meat into the remaining Cumberland glaze.

Over the past few years hog roasting has become increasingly popular. You'll find them at all sorts of outdoor summer events.

A whole hog is actually a very easy thing to cook, but it does need some rather specialist equipment. Hog or pig roasters come in many guises. They're often gas powered and can range from small suckling pigs spits to larger 2 x 50kg rotating machines that you tow behind your car. See Resources on page 218 for hire companies – some even provide a chef to oversee the cooking and carving of the meat.

I use an open fire roaster, purely because I can then vary the fuel source from charcoal lumps to briquettes and even seasoned split logs, to add a smoky flavour.

There really is no definitive recipe here, it's really down to common sense, and a long cooking time. It's a bit daunting at the start I grant you, but after a couple of times you will, like any cooking get a feel for it, and once you have tasted the incredible flavours you can produce from a few simple ingredients, you will want to cook all year round.

Hog Roasting

Rather than write a recipe here, I'm going to give you a few pointers that will be helpful. The first thing is to check the manufacturer's instructions as to the limit on total weight that the motor can take. Next, make sure any piece of meat whole or butchered will not only fit on the spit, but will also be secure and not fall off once cooked.

Start the fires a good 30 minutes before you want to start cooking, so the meat will seal straight away – always a good thing in warm weather.

A good rule to see if the fire is hot enough, is to hold your hand roughly where the food will be cooked – you should be able to count up to about seven or eight before having to remove your hand.

For whole pigs, I secure well to the spit well with the forks provided, then season really well with salt and pepper, inside and out. I then score the skin really well with a Stanley knife at regular intervals, so the fat can be released, this will ensure beautiful crackling.

Next, is to keep an eye on the heat, re-fuel when the charcoal or wood is half burnt, this will ensure an even heat source. If you let the heat go right down, it takes a good 30 minutes to get back to the original temperature.

I like to baste hog roasts simply with the cooking juices from the meat. The constant basting process really adds a fabulous flavour. I sometimes brush the meat with a little olive oil, but nothing more is needed. Or if you prefer you can add a dry spice rub before cooking.

Cooking times are really important. For 12kg of meat I would allow 3–4 hours, 25kg meat 4–6 hours and 50kg meat 8–9 hours, but the final cooking time is dependent on a variety of factors such as temperature, heat source, fuel used, maintaining a careful eye and so on.

Do remember to be careful – these things get incredibly hot so be aware of kids as well as adults who have had a couple of drinks!

Here is the first of my home-smoked recipes. All the recipes on the next few pages are cooked in a Bradley smoker (see Resources on page 218 for more details).

This salmon dish is really wonderful, it takes a little time to smoke but it is well worth the wait. I generally like my fish lightly cooked, so I usually smoke it for 1–2 hours, but you can leave it for as long or as little as you like.

Sweet Mirin Smoked Salmon

SERVES 4 • PREPARATION TIME 10 MINUTES • SMOKING TIME 1–2 HOURS

4 x 250g salmon fillets, skin on
150g sachet good-quality
    teriyaki sauce
2 tbsp caster sugar
4 tbsp *mirin* (Chinese rice wine)
new potatoes, to serve

You will need a Bradley smoker
    or similar

Preheat the smoker to 120°C.

Place the salmon in a bowl. Mix the remaining ingredients together in a jug and stir well. Pour two-thirds of the sauce over the fish, turning to coat it thoroughly.

Place the salmon fillets into two small disposable barbecue trays. Smoke until the salmon is just cooked (1–2 hours) – do not let it overcook or it will become tough.

Serve warm with a little of the reserved sauce and new potatoes.

Hot Spiced Smoked Brisket

SERVES 6–8 • **PREPARATION TIME** 20 MINUTES PLUS OVERNIGHT MARINATING • **SMOKING TIME** 5–6 HOURS

Hot smoked brisket is a delicious meal at any time of the year. There are many unwritten rules on the best way to prepare, smoke and eat this magnificent dish. But my method is fairly straightforward – it just takes time, and a lot of patience – you definitely cannot rush this dish! But I know you're going to enjoy the end results, they are so worth waiting for!

2.5kg piece brisket, with fat on, about 5–6cm thick at the thickest part

For the spice rub

3 tbsp sea salt

3 tbsp unrefined brown sugar

3 tbsp black peppercorns, *cracked*

2 tbsp paprika

1 tbsp dried chilli flakes

3 tbsp garlic granules

2 tbsp ground cumin

For the marinade

100ml cider vinegar

50ml extra virgin olive oil

2 tbsp Worcestershire Sauce

2 onions, *roughly chopped*

You will need a Bradley smoker or similar

Place all the ingredients for the spice rub in a medium bowl and stir well to combine.

Place all the marinade ingredients into a liquidiser or food processor, add 150ml water and blitz to a fine basting sauce. Add one third of the spice rub to the marinade and mix really well. Place the brisket in a glass, ceramic or stainless steel tray.

Place half the remaining dry spice mixture on to the meat and rub it in really well. Carefully turn the joint over and rub the remaining spice mixture in. Cover and chill overnight.

Preheat the smoker to 110°C.

Spoon about 6 tablespoons of the marinade over the meat and then place the tray in the smoker. Smoke for 1 hour, then turn the meat over and baste it with another 6 tablespoons of the marinade. Return the tray to the smoker and repeat the turning and basting process every hour for the next 5–6 hours. You will find that over the cooking period, juices will run from the beef – I just keep basting them over.

After 5 hours, check to see if the meat is cooked – try to push your finger through the beef – it should go through with a slight resistance. If not, then smoke it for another hour.

Once cooked, remove from the smoker, wrap the whole tray in foil and leave the joint to rest for 20 minutes.

Slice and serve warm.

This will keep for up to 1 week in the fridge. Slices of the beef can be gently reheated in a microwave, covered with clingfilm, for 2–3 minutes; or in a preheated oven at 180°C/gas mark 4, wrapped in foil, for 15 minutes.

I think turkey must be one the most under-used meats around. It's very versatile and you can pair it with almost any spice, herb or sweet flavour. One of my favourite ways to cook turkey is to smoke it over a long period of time, thus ensuring it stays delicious and moist. Turkey legs are just perfect for smoking. In fact I'd be surprised if you ever eat a juicier piece of meat than these delicious maple syrup glazed turkey legs! All you need is time, a little patience and a few key ingredients.

Hot Smoked Maple Syrup Glazed Turkey Legs

SERVES 4–6 • **PREPARATION TIME** 20 MINUTES PLUS OVERNIGHT SALTING • **COOKING TIME** 5–8 HOURS PLUS REGULAR BASTING

2 turkey legs, about 950g each

6 tbsp sea salt

2 tbsp maple syrup

For the spice rub

1 tbsp paprika

1 tbsp ground cumin

1 tbsp ground cinnamon

½ tbsp ground turmeric

1 tbsp dried garlic granules

For the glaze

150ml maple syrup

juice of 1 small orange

juice of 2 large limes

2 tbsp white wine vinegar

1½ tbsp cornflour

freshly ground black pepper

You will need a Bradley smoker or similar

Carefully chop the knuckle end off the turkey legs. Wash and thoroughly dry the legs, then place them in a glass, ceramic or stainless steel tray. Sprinkle the sea salt over the turkey legs and rub it in really well. Spoon over the maple syrup and rub that in really well too. Cover and place in the fridge overnight.

The next day, place all the ingredients for the spice rub in a small bowl, stir well to combine. Place all the ingredients for the glaze in a jug add 2 tablespoons water, season with black pepper and stir well.

Preheat the smoker to 110°C.

Rinse the turkey legs well under cold running water and pat dry with kitchen paper. Wash the tray and return the legs to the tray. Spoon the spice mixture all over the legs and rub it in really well.

Place the tray into the smoker and smoke the legs for 30 minutes. At this point brush the legs thoroughly with the glaze, turn over and brush again. Repeat every 30 minutes for the next 5 hours, if possible – the longer the better. The cooked legs will be a beautiful colour and very moist indeed.

Once cooked, carefully remove the tray from the smoker. Wrap the whole tray in foil and leave for 20 minutes to rest. Slice and serve warm.

I sometimes find it hard to believe that something as simple as smoking can produce such amazing results. This is definitely one of those recipes – it produces slightly shrivelled tomatoes which have an intense sweet yet subtle, smoky flavour.

These tomatoes can be used as a side dish, in a salad, thrown into pasta... the possibilities are endless!

Sweet and Sour Smoked Tomatoes

SERVES 6–8 • PREPARATION TIME 10 MINUTES • SMOKING TIME 5 HOURS

16 large, ripe, well-perfumed
   tomatoes
4–5 tbsp balsamic vinegar
4–5 tbsp caster sugar
2–3 tbsp olive oil
olive oil, for brushing
salt and freshly ground black pepper

You will need a Bradley smoker
   or similar

Preheat the smoker to 190°C.

Cut the tomatoes in half horizontally and place them skin-side down on a baking tray. Carefully spoon a little vinegar over all the tomato halves. Sprinkle a little sugar and salt and pepper over all the tomatoes.

Place the tray in the smoker and smoke the tomatoes for 5 hours.

Once cooked, brush well with the oil, cool and chill well.

Herby Smoked Olive Oil

MAKES 500ML • PREPARATION TIME 10 MINUTES PLUS OVERNIGHT MARINATING • SMOKING TIME 2 HOURS

This is a lovely way to get a deliciously smoky flavour in a variety of foods. I have given the timings to make a lightly smoked oil. You can smoke it for a longer or shorter period of time for a more or less intense flavour - just see what you fancy. Use sparingly as the oil will have a very pungent, smoky flavour.

500ml extra virgin olive oil
1 small bunch of fresh thyme
6 sprigs of fresh rosemary
1 garlic bulb, *roughly chopped*

You will need a Bradley smoker
   or similar

The day before you are planning to smoke the oil, place the olive oil, herbs and garlic into a large bowl and mix really well. Cover and leave to marinate overnight at room temperature.

The next day, preheat the smoker to 80°C.

Place the oil, herbs and garlic in a shallow tray. Place in the smoker and smoke for 2 hours. Keep an eye on the temperature to ensure it stays around 80°C. After 2 hours, remove, cool and store in a fridge.

Sweet Chilli Hot Smoked Squash

SERVES 4–6 • PREPARATION TIME 15 MINUTES • SMOKING TIME 5–6 HOURS

I like to smoke lots of different types of vegetables. Sometimes I'll lightly smoke some veg then finish them off in the oven without smoke - it's a very versatile way of cooking and preserving foods.

Smoked squash really makes a great difference to the flavour of a dish - try in soups, broths or even a salsa or dip. Once smoked the flesh will freeze really well for up to 1 month.

2 medium butternut squash, *cut into 8 pieces lengthways, seeds removed*
2 tsp dried chilli flakes
4 tbsp olive oil
4 level tbsp clear honey
extra olive oil, *for brushing*
salt and freshly ground black pepper

You will need a Bradley smoker
   or similar

Line a baking tray with baking parchment (this makes it much easier to clean afterwards!).

Place the pieces of squash on the lined tray. Mix the chilli, oil and honey together, then brush it on to the squash. Season well with salt and pepper.

Place in the smoker and smoke for 1 hour, then check and brush with oil. Check and brush the squash every hour or until it is cooked through.

Ice Cream Oysters and
Ice Cream Wafer Sandwiches

There really is no real recipe here, just to say buy good-quality ice cream and sandwich away. On childhood holidays in Blackpool my father always enjoyed an 'oyster' from a small ice-cream van on the seafront.

They bring back such fond memories for me, even to the extent that I recently bought an antique ice cream block maker from the States so I could have the wonderful marshmallow ice cream wafer sandwiches.as well. Most of the supermarkets now sell them again.

Sometimes you just have to have a laugh with food and this really is a giggle! It looks spectacular, just pile on as much and as many different colours and flavours of ice cream as possible! It's ideal for children's birthday parties.

You will need a giant cupcake tin – see page 218 for stockists or check yur local kitchen shop.

Giant Ice Cream Cupcake

SERVES • PREPARATION TIME 20 MINUTES PLUS OVERNIGHT CHILLING • **COOKING TIME** 50 MINUTES

For the cake

butter, for greasing

350g unsalted butter, *softened*

350g caster sugar

6 medium eggs, at room temperature

350g self-raising flour

a selection of ice cream

For the icing

8 tbsp fondant icing sugar

finely grated zest and juice of
   1 large lime

Preheat the oven to 160°C/gas mark 3. Lightly grease the giant cupcake tin with the butter.

Place the butter and sugar in a large mixing bowl and beat them together until light and fluffy. Gradually add the eggs, until they are all incorporated. Finally, add the flour and mix, but do not overbeat.

Spoon roughly three-quarters of the mix into the base of the giant cupcake tin and cook in the oven for 10 minutes.

Next add the rest of the mix into the lid of the cupcake tin and cook for a further 40 minutes, or until set and lightly browned. Once cooked, leave to cool in the tin for 10 minutes to set before trying to turn out. This sets the sponge nicely.

Remove from the tin, then chill overnight.

With a sharp knife, carefully cut around the edge of the bottom half of the cup cake, leaving a 1cm gap. Remove all the sponge, then place the lid in a cereal bowl and do the same. Fill the bottom of the cake with small balls of various ice creams. Top with the lid and freeze for 10 minutes.

Make up the fondant icing by mixing the sugar, lime zest and juice.

Remove the cake from the freezer and drizzle over the fondant icing. Serve straight away.

Chapter 9
SAUCES, SALADS & SIDES

No outdoor book would be complete without a selection of accompaniments such as sauces, salads, dips and sides. The dishes here work well with all barbecue food and the salads make perfect picnic food, too. This section showcases some of my favourite recipes, many from my time spent in the southern states of America researching not only barbecues but also their wonderful sauces, glazes and rubs. I hope you'll be inspired to give the more unusual ones a whirl, such as fried green tomatoes and my version of the famous American chopped salad – a satisfying meal in itself.

There is nothing worse than going to a barbecue and seeing the same old salads, potatoes and bought-in dressings and sauces. So take the opportunity to wow your guests with some real crackers!

Simple and so good. Everybody needs a good salsa recipe up their sleeve to serve with burgers and all manner of barbecued foods.

Simple Tomato Salsa

SERVES 4–6 • PREPARATION TIME 15 MINUTES

12 cherry tomatoes, *quartered*
4 garlic cloves, *finely chopped*
2 tsp finely chopped fresh red chilli
1 small red onion, *very finely chopped*
4 tbsp extra virgin olive oil
3 tbsp sherry vinegar
4 tbsp snipped fresh chives
salt and freshly ground black pepper

Place the chopped tomatoes, garlic, chilli, onion, oil, vinegar, chives into a bowl and mix well.

Season well with salt and pepper. Chill and serve.

A nice fresh salsa – easy to make and it makes a particularly great accompaniment to burgers.

If you can't get hold of a fresh pineapple, simply use canned pineapple instead – it will be just as good.

Chilli Pineapple Salsa

SERVES 4–6 • PREPARATION TIME 15 MINUTES

1 small, very ripe golden pineapple
2 pinches dried chilli flakes
1 red pepper, *deseeded and finely chopped*
2 spring onions, *very finely chopped*
finely grated zest and juice of 3 large limes
4 tbsp roughly chopped fresh coriander
1 tbsp very finely chopped fresh ginger
2 tbsp clear honey
salt and freshly ground black pepper

Top and tail the pineapple. Carefully peel it with a sharp knife. Cut it into slices, remove the woody core and finely chop the flesh. Place in a serving dish.

Add the remaining ingredients to the dish, including a generous seasoning of salt and black pepper. Mix well, cover and chill for 1 hour before serving.

Mango, Cucumber and Coriander Relish

SERVES 4–6 • PREPARATION TIME 15 MINUTES
PLUS MARINATING

This is a lovely combination of fresh, tangy ingredients that makes a fab side to serve with grilled fish such as tuna, bream or salmon. As with all relishes it's best left for an hour or two to marinate and it will keep for 2–3 days.

2 large ripe mangoes
1 red pepper, *deseeded and finely diced*
½ small cucumber
6 spring onions
4 tbsp chopped fresh coriander
finely grated zest and juice of 3 large limes
2 tbsp clear honey
salt and freshly ground black pepper

Remove the flesh from the mango, by slicing down the fruit with a sharp knife to remove it from the oval shaped stone. If the mango is ripe enough you can remove the soft flesh from the skin with a dessertspoon, then chop it finely. Transfer the chopped mango and any juice to a serving dish.

Add the diced pepper to the mango pieces. Cut the cucumber into 4 strips, then slice finely, add to the mango and pepper and mix well.

Slice the spring onions on the diagonal, and add to the mango and the peppers. Add the coriander, lime zest and juice, honey and plenty of seasoning.

Chill for 1–2 hours, then check the seasoning and serve.

Watermelon Salsa

SERVES 4–6 • PREPARATION TIME 20 MINUTES
PLUS CHILLING

This crisp, light salsa goes with most barbecued meats or fish. If you can prepare it in advance and chill it for a couple of hours then the flavours are even better!

½ small watermelon, *skinned, deseeded and cut into small dice*
1 small red onion, *very finely chopped*
1 tsp finely chopped fresh red chilli
4 tomatoes, *cut into small dice*
2 tbsp roughly chopped fresh coriander
2 tbsp chopped fresh mint
2 tbsp red wine vinegar
3–4 tsp caster sugar
finely grated zest and juice of 2 large limes
salt and freshly ground black pepper

Place the watermelon, onion, chilli, tomatoes, coriander and mint in a serving bowl and really mix well.

Place the vinegar, sugar, lime zest and juice and salt and pepper in a jug and stir well.

Pour the vinegar mixture over the melon and tomato mixture and stir well. Chill well, for at least 1 hour.

When you are ready to serve the salsa, check the seasoning and adjust if needed with salt and pepper, the sugar and vinegar balance may need tweaking slightly too. Serve well chilled within 2–3 hours of making.

The intensity of the flavours here is really delicious – the horseradish and sweet chilli work really well together. If you can leave it to marinate for 24 hours then all the better, but it's really difficult keeping your hands off, believe me!

I like to serve this as a starter nibble or with grilled or barbecued meats or fish.

Pickled Corn Rings with Sweet Chilli and Horseradish

SERVES 4–6 • PREPARATION TIME 20 MINUTES PLUS MARINATING • COOKING TIME 6 MINUTES

300ml white wine vinegar

2 garlic cloves, *crushed*

4 tbsp ready-made sweet chilli sauce

6 tbsp unrefined granulated sugar

12 cloves

3 tbsp sea salt

2 medium corn on the cob, *cut into 1cm rounds*

1 small red onion, *cut into thin wedges*

3 tbsp salted capers, *rinsed well*

150ml good-quality olive oil

1 tbsp creamed horseradish

crusty bread, to serve

Place the vinegar, garlic, chilli sauce, sugar, cloves, salt and 200ml cold water into a medium stainless steel pan, stir and bring to the boil, then simmer for 3 minutes.

Add the corn slices and simmer for a further 2 minutes.

Place the onion and capers into a glass, ceramic or stainless steel bowl. Pour the hot pickle and corn mixture carefully over the onions and capers. Stir well.

Finally add the olive oil and creamed horseradish and mix well. Cool uncovered, then cover and chill overnight or for up to 24 hours.

Drain and eat using your fingers – crusty bread dipped into the marinade is delicious.

The real must here is to make sure the avocados are ripe – it just doesn't work with under-ripe avocado. If the avocados you buy are rock hard, place them in a paper bag with a banana. Leave them at room temperature for 24-48 hours and they will magically ripen.

I like to serve a spoonful of guacamole with salmon. Simply grill a salmon steak with a little butter or olive oil and plenty of salt and pepper for a few minutes on each side (do not overcook) then serve with a spoonful of the guacamole and a few minted new potatoes.

Guacamole

SERVES 4 • PREPARATION TIME 15 MINUTES

2 ripe avocados, *halved and stoned*

2 small shallots, *finely chopped*

2 garlic cloves, *crushed*

1–2 tsp sherry vinegar

2 small, ripe tomatoes, *roughly chopped*

1–2 tbsp extra virgin olive oil

juice of 1 large lime

2 tbsp chopped fresh coriander

salt and freshly ground pepper

breadsticks, crackers, tortillas or even poppadoms, to serve

Using a dessertspoon, scoop out the avocado flesh, put it into a bowl and break it up using a fork. Next add the shallots, garlic, vinegar and chopped tomatoes and mix well. Then add the oil, lime juice, coriander and plenty of salt and pepper and mix well. Transfer to a serving bowl and serve within 1 hour.

Serve the guacamole at room temperature with breadsticks, crackers, tortillas or even poppadoms.

Here is my take on a North Carolina-style barbecue sauce, which can be used as a dipping sauce for cooked meats and vegetables. Cook it for a little longer and it goes slightly thicker – then you have a dip for tortillas or nachos or a marinade to brush over meat during barbecuing or grilling.

Carolina-style Barbecue Sauce

SERVES 6–8 • PREPARATION TIME 10 MINUTES • COOKING TIME 15 MINUTES

100ml olive oil

1 medium onion, *finely chopped*

1 red pepper, *finely chopped*

2 garlic cloves, *chopped*

125ml tomato ketchup

175ml passata

3 tbsp cider vinegar

6 tbsp Worcestershire Sauce

juice of 1 lemon

150ml pineapple juice

2 tsp Tabasco Sauce

1 tbsp black treacle

3 tbsp light brown sugar

3 tbsp Dijon mustard

1 tsp English mustard powder

1 tsp ground black pepper

1 tsp sea salt

Heat the olive oil in a medium pan and add the onion, red pepper and garlic. Cook for 3 minutes to soften slightly.

Add the rest of the ingredients and bring to the boil. Turn down the heat and simmer for 10 minutes to thicken, or until the desired consistency is reached. Keep warm and serve.

This will keep for up to 1 week in the fridge.

My Barbecue Sauce

SERVES 8 • PREPARATION TIME 10 MINUTES •
COOKING TIME 20 MINUTES

This is my lighter version of barbecue sauce. It will keep for a week or two in the fridge.

100ml olive oil

2 medium onions, *finely chopped*

4 garlic cloves, *chopped*

200ml tomato ketchup

200ml passata

50ml cider vinegar

100ml Worcestershire Sauce

juice of 3 large lemons

150ml pineapple juice

150ml apple juice

4 tbsp light brown sugar

4 tbsp English mustard

1 tsp ground black pepper

1 vegetable stock cube, *crumbled*

1 tbsp cornflour or arrowroot

Heat the olive oil in a medium pan and add the onions and garlic. Cook for 3 minutes to soften slightly.

Add the remaining ingredients (except the cornflour or arrowroot) to the pan and bring to the boil. Turn down the heat and simmer for 10 minutes.

I like to thicken my sauce slightly, as it can sometimes separate. I do this by mixing the cornflour or arrowroot with 2 tablespoons of cold water and stirring it into the simmering sauce, it will thicken almost immediately.

Check the seasoning and adjust if needed. Keep warm and serve or transfer to a jug, cool, cover and chill.

Carolina-Style Chilli Dipping Sauce

SERVES 6–8 • PREPARATION TIME 10 MINUTES

This is an all-round good sauce for dipping, marinating or brushing over barbecued meats. There's no cooking involved and it's simply a case of mixing all the ingredients together – couldn't be easier!

250ml cider vinegar

250ml white wine vinegar

300ml water

200ml tomato ketchup

75g dark brown sugar

4 level tsp dried chilli flakes

75ml olive oil

salt

Combine all the ingredients, except the salt, in a large jug. Add 300ml water, stir well to combine and season to taste with salt.

Cover and store in the fridge for up to 1 month.

Pinto Bean, Bacon and Tomato Dip

SERVES 4–6 • PREPARATION TIME 10 MINUTES • COOKING TIME 20–30 MINUTES

Pinto beans are delicious and make a great-dip-come-side-dish. If you cannot find them, then use cannellini, borlotti or even kidney beans. The bacon adds a nice meaty kick to the beans, but you can omit for a vegetarian version – just add a couple of tablespoons of olive oil to the pan to cook the onions in. This is best cooked and cooled, then gently reheated or eaten cold with tortillas and a glass of beer.

225g streaky bacon, *finely chopped*

1 tsp finely chopped fresh red chilli

2 garlic cloves, *finely chopped*

2 small red onions, *very finely chopped*

2 x 400g cans pinto beans, *drained and rinsed well*

1 vegetable stock cube, *crumbled*

400g can chopped tomatoes

2 tsp sugar

salt and freshly ground black pepper

Heat a saucepan, then add the bacon, chilli, garlic and onions and cook until the fat comes out of the bacon and the onions start to colour slightly.

Add the beans, stock cube, tomatoes, sugar and 300ml water and season with salt and pepper. Gently simmer for 20–30 minutes or until thick and chunky.

Transfer the dip to an airtight container, cool, cover and chill until ready to serve.

Cumberland Glaze

SERVES 6–8 • PREPARATION TIME 15 MINUTES • COOKING TIME 10 MINUTES

This is great as a glaze for barbecued game such as hare (see page 165), but I also like it brushed over beef short ribs or even lamb ribs.

1 large orange

1 large lemon

400g redcurrant jelly

100ml port

pinch of mixed spice

1 tbsp arrowroot

Remove the zest carefully from the orange and lemon using a vegetable peeler and then cut it into very thin strips. Place the zest in a small pan, cover it with cold water and bring to the boil. Strain the zest and repeat the procedure twice more, then drain the zest well.

Meanwhile squeeze the juice from the orange and lemon and place it in a medium pan. Add the jelly, port and mixed spice. Bring to the boil and simmer for 1 minute, then add the cooked, drained zests, and continue to cook for 5–6 minutes to thicken slightly.

Blend the arrowroot with 2 tbsp cold water, stir well and add it, a little at a time, to the simmering sauce. It will thicken immediately; don't go mad, it should be thick enough to coat the back of a spoon nicely. Remove from the heat and set aside to cool.

This will keep for up to 1 month in the fridge.

I like the flavour here but also the beautiful colour. It's great served with burgers, chops and even slow-cooked meats.

Roast Pumpkin, Sweet Chilli and Rocket Dip

SERVES 4–6 • **PREPARATION TIME** 20 MINUTES • **COOKING TIME** 30 MINUTES

400g pumpkin or squash, *cut into small chunks*

1 red onion, *finely sliced*

3 garlic cloves

8 tbsp olive oil

3 tbsp balsamic vinegar

2 tsp caster sugar

¼ tsp dried chilli flakes

50g rocket

75g pumpkin seeds

salt and freshly ground black pepper

Preheat the oven to 220°C/gas mark 7.

Place the pumpkin or squash, onion, garlic, 4 tablespoons of the olive oil, vinegar, sugar and chilli flakes in a bowl and mix well. Season well with salt and pepper. Place the mixture in a large baking tin, then pop into the oven. Cook for 25–30 minutes, until the mixture is well browned and cooked through.

Carefully transfer the cooked mixture into a food processor. Add the rocket and the remaining oil, then process until you have a chunky purée – it shouldn't be too fine.

Spoon the dip into a bowl, stir in the seeds, check the seasoning and adjust if needed. Cover and store in the fridge for up to 3 days.

White Apple Dipping Sauce

SERVES 4–6 • PREPARATION TIME 10 MINUTES

This idea came from the wonderful 'Big Bob Gibson's BBQ Book'. The recipe originally came from Alabama, USA and is a cross between a dipping sauce and a basting sauce. It's quite unusual to see a white sauce on a barbecue but it makes a nice change, has a great flavour and as a bonus is very simple to make.

400g mayonnaise

2 tbsp creamed horseradish

1 tbsp Dijon mustard

200ml apple juice

finely grated zest and juice of 2 large limes

pinch or two of chilli powder

salt and freshly ground black pepper

Simply place all the ingredients in a mixing bowl and stir them really well until thoroughly combined. Taste and adjust the seasoning if necessary.

Cover and store in the fridge for up to 2 days.

Dry Sherry Dipping Sauce

SERVES 4 • PREPARATION TIME 10 MINUTES
PLUS 15 MINUTES INFUSING

This is great with the Prawn Burgers (see page 30) but is also pretty good with grilled duck or the Turkey Burgers (page 27).

150ml dry sherry

zest and juice of 2 oranges

4 tbsp dark soy sauce

2 tbsp finely grated fresh ginger

2 tbsp sherry vinegar

½ tsp very finely chopped fresh red chilli

1 garlic clove, *very finely chopped*

2 spring onions, *finely sliced on the diagonal*

½ tsp ground black pepper

2 tsp caster sugar

Combine all the ingredients in a serving jug, stir well to combine and leave to infuse for at least 15 minutes.

Just before serving the sauce, give it a good stir.

I first tasted this delicious veg medley in New Zealand in 1985 and I've been cooking it ever since. I had it on a very large burger called a kitchen sink, meaning that it had everything thrown on. It's not too dissimilar to piccalilli and it makes a tangy, colourful accompaniment to any barbecued meat, fish or vegetables. The secret is not to overcook the vegetables.

Chow Chow

SERVES 8–10 • PREPARATION TIME 30 MINUTES PLUS OVERNIGHT SALTING • COOKING TIME 15–20 MINUTES

½ medium cucumber, *finely chopped*

400g green beans (runners or flat beans are best), *finely chopped*

400g celery, *chopped into small pieces*

1 small cauliflower, *broken into small florets*

½ large white cabbage, *very finely chopped*

400g green tomatoes, *finely chopped, optional*

3 tbsp salt

275g caster sugar

5 heaped tbsp English mustard powder

1 tbsp turmeric

6–7 heaped tbsp plain flour

1 tsp ground white pepper

1 tbsp poppy seeds or kalonji seeds, optional

1.2 litres malt vinegar

salt and freshly ground black pepper

Place all the vegetables into a large bowl and mix well. Add the salt and mix really well again, then place the vegetables into a colander over the bowl and chill well overnight.

In the morning you'll see the liquid that has been drawn out of the vegetables. Discard the liquid and rinse the veg well under cold water, then drain well.

Place the sugar, mustard powder, turmeric, flour, pepper and seeds together into a bowl and add a little vinegar to form a loose paste.

Place the rest of the vinegar and all the vegetables into a stainless steel pan, bring to the simmer. At this point, stir through the mustard paste and bring to a simmer again and the mix will thicken.

Turn the heat down and simmer for about 10 minutes, or until the vegetables are cooked but still have a little bite.

Leave to cool, season to taste and then chill well.

Keep in the fridge for up to 2 months.

Coriander, Apricot and Fig Stuffing

SERVES 8–10 • PREPARATION TIME 20 MINUTES
• COOKING TIME 15 MINUTES

This is great with Christmas Turkey on a Charcoal Barbecue (see page 164) but is also good with roast chicken, pork or duck. If you prefer to serve the stuffing separately, pop it into a buttered ovenproof dish and cook it in a preheated oven at 180°C/gas mark 4 for 20–30 minutes.

2 tbsp vegetable oil
1 medium onion, *finely chopped*
1 garlic clove, *finely chopped*
1 tbsp dried thyme
500g sausagemeat
1 medium egg
6–8 tbsp dried natural breadcrumbs
75g semi-dried apricots
175g semi-dried figs
4 tbsp roughly chopped fresh coriander
salt and freshly ground black pepper

Heat the oil in a medium pan, add the onion and garlic and cook for a few minutes until soft and translucent. Add the thyme and sausagemeat and stir well, just break down the sausagemeat but do not actually cook it through. Set aside to cool slightly.

Add the egg and enough breadcrumbs to the sausagemeat mixture to stiffen it up, but remember they will continue to thicken as they reconstitute themselves so take care not to add too many.

Finally, add the apricots, figs and coriander, season and mix well. Use as required.

Gin and Cranberry Relish

SERVES 6–8 • PREPARATION TIME 15 MINUTES
• COOKING TIME 35–40 MINUTES

This works really well with most rich food as well as the roast turkey on page 163.

2 tbsp vegetable oil
2 heaped tsp cumin seeds
2 tbsp kalonji seeds
2 tsp freshly grated nutmeg
2 large onions, *finely chopped*
2 garlic cloves, *crushed*
2 x 75g packets dried cranberries
75g packet dried cherries
75g packet dried blueberries
100g caster sugar
100ml red wine vinegar
100ml gin
6 tbsp olive oil
salt and freshly ground black pepper

Heat the oil in a stainless steel pan. Add the cumin, kalonji seeds and nutmeg and stir around in the hot oil to release their wonderful aroma, but do not burn. Add the onions and continue to cook for 2–3 minutes. Add the garlic and cook for a further 1 minute. Add the dried fruits and sugar, season and stir well. Pour in the vinegar along with 300ml cold water and bring to the boil, then turn down the heat and simmer gently for about 25 minutes.

When nearly all the liquid has evaporated, check the seasoning and adjust if necessary. Remove the pan from the heat and stir in the olive oil. Spoon the relish into a Kilner or screw-top jar and leave to mature for about 1 week.

Quick Roasted Red Pepper Aïoli

SERVES 4–6 • PREPARATION TIME 15 MINUTES • COOKING TIME 20 MINUTES

Aïoli I think must have a really pungent garlic kick, and the best way to achieve this is to leave the garlic as fresh as possible. So soften the onions, then blitz well with the peppers and add the raw garlic.

No seasoning is really needed, just a dash of vinegar and a little black pepper if you are using ready-made mayonnaise. This will go with all burgers, but is especially good with fresh tuna, turkey or chicken burgers.

2 tbsp olive oil
½ small onion, *finely chopped*
280g jar roasted red peppers, *well drained*
2 garlic cloves, *finely chopped*
225g mayonnaise (you may not need all of it)
dash of any vinegar
freshly ground black pepper

Heat the oil in a small frying pan, then add the onion and cook for 10 minutes over a fairly high heat until it softens and takes on a nice colour. Add the peppers, stir well and cook for a further 10 minutes. Set aside to cool.

Transfer the onion and peppers to a food processor, add the garlic and blitz until you have a thick purée. Add enough mayonnaise to make a thick, beautifully red sauce.

Season with a dash of vinegar and pepper. Chill in the fridge until needed.

Carolina-style Coleslaw

SERVES 6 • PREPARATION TIME 15 MINUTES

Not a true authentic Carolina coleslaw, but delicious nevertheless. Simply add the light dressing to the chopped veg and leave for 30 minutes, stirring occasionally.

250g white cabbage, *very finely sliced*
250g red cabbage, *very finely sliced*
1 large, sweet onion, *very finely sliced*

For the dressing
125ml cider vinegar
125ml white wine vinegar
250ml water
100ml tomato ketchup
40g dark brown sugar
2 level tsp dried chilli flakes
50ml olive oil
salt

Thoroughly mix the sliced cabbages and onion together in a serving bowl.

Mix the remaining ingredients together in a jug and stir well. Pour the dressing over the cabbage and mix all the ingredients together well. Cover and set aside for the flavours to develop for 30 minutes.

Check the seasoning, you may need to add a little salt before serving.

Basically anything goes in this salad. I had a cracker recently at Atlanta airport, and I liked the fact that I felt really full and satisfied after I'd eaten a salad. I like to add ham to mine plus plenty of dressing. The important thing to remember is to chop the ingredients as small as possible. The end result should be really packed full of texture and flavour.

Prepare this no more than an hour in advance.

American-style Chopped Salad

SERVES 4 • PREPARATION TIME 20 MINUTES

4 small, ripe tomatoes

½ large cucumber

1 iceberg lettuce

4 shallots

2 large carrots, *peeled*

4 tbsp honey-roast peanuts,
   finely chopped

4 hard-boiled eggs, *finely chopped*

4 tbsp snipped fresh chives

200g wafer thin ham, chicken
   or turkey

For the dressing

3 tbsp extra virgin olive oil

3 tbsp safflower or sunflower oil

4 tbsp red wine vinegar

2 tbsp Dijon mustard

1 tsp caster sugar

salt and freshly ground black pepper

Slice and chop the tomatoes. Place them in a large serving dish. Deseed the cucumber with a teaspoon, then very finely slice and chop into pieces the same size as the tomato flesh. Add to the dish.

Next, finely slice the lettuce and shallots and add them to the tomatoes and cucumber. Finely slice the carrots, then chop the slices into pieces the same size as the tomatoes and add to the dish.

Finally add the nuts, chopped eggs, chives and the meat. Mix together really well, cover and chill.

Meanwhile, make the dressing by placing all the ingredients into a bowl and whisking together. After a couple of minutes, the mustard will emulsify the oil and vinegar and you will end up with a thickish dressing.

If you are planning to eat the salad straight away, pour the dressing over the salad and mix really well. Season with salt and pepper and serve.

If you are going to serve it later then pour the dressing over the salad and season at the last moment.

Thai-style Spicy Carrot Salad

SERVES 2 • PREPARATION TIME 15 MINUTES
PLUS MARINATING

This crisp, tasty salad makes a great starter or accompaniment to roasted corn-fed chicken breasts.

1 lemon
100g green beans, *cut into 2cm pieces*
10 cherry plum tomatoes, *halved*
2 medium organic carrots, *peeled*
¼ white cabbage

For the dressing
juice of 3 large limes
3 tbsp tamarind paste
3 tbsp *nam pla* (Thai fish sauce)
2 garlic cloves, *finely chopped*
2 heaped tsp finely chopped fresh red chilli
3 tbsp light soy sauce
1 heaped tbsp caster sugar
50ml vegetable oil
salt and freshly ground black pepper, optional

Cut 8 paper-thin slices from the lemon and cut these into quarters. Place the lemon quarters, beans and tomatoes into a large bowl. Finely slice the carrots and cabbage in the food processor. Add to the bowl and mix well.

Place all the dressing ingredients, apart from the oil and salt, in a medium jug and mix well. Finally add the oil in a thin stream and mix well. Pour the dressing over the salad, mix well and taste and season if needed. Set aside for 20 minutes, at room temperature, then stir again and serve.

Sweet and Sour Tamarind Cucumber Relish

SERVES 4 • PREPARATION TIME 15 MINUTES
PLUS FREEZING, DRAINING AND STANDING

The key here is to freeze the cucumbers solid first. This breaks down the cell structure, making the strips of cucumber really pliable.

2 large cucumbers, *frozen whole, then defrosted, dried and cut into ½cm-thick long strips*
2 pinches of salt

For the dressing
5 tbsp rice wine vinegar
3 tbsp tamarind paste
2 tbsp *mirin* (Chinese rice wine)
1 tbsp clear honey
2 tbsp olive oil
1 tbsp kalonji seeds
1 garlic clove, *crushed*
1 small red onion, *very finely chopped*
4 tbsp finely chopped pickled ginger
salt and freshly ground black pepper

Sprinkle salt over the prepared cucumber strips, mix well and leave to drain for 20 minutes. This toughens up the strips and removes a little more moisture. Rinse well in cold water to remove the salt and pat dry again. Place the slices in a serving bowl.

Mix all the ingredients for the dressing together in a medium jug, then pour over the cucumber and mix well. Season to taste if necessary – you may not need any salt. Allow to stand for 20 minutes before serving.

This salad is a communal salad, by which I mean you make it up and serve it in a large bowl in the middle of the table, for everyone to tuck into. Served inside or outside it's a really filling, super-tasty salad.

I like to serve this on its own with rice crackers or as an accompaniment to fish or lightly grilled meats.

Warm Mixed Beans and Potatoes with Gorgonzola Dressing

SERVES 6–8 • **PREPARATION TIME** 25 MINUTES • **COOKING TIME** 10–15 MINUTES

250g baby new potatoes, *skin on and halved*

50g frozen baby broad beans

½ small fennel bulb, *very finely shaved*

410g can borlotti beans, *rinsed and well drained*

410g can butter beans, *rinsed and well drained*

410g can cannellini beans, *rinsed and well drained*

6 tbsp olive oil

1 head romaine lettuce, *finely shredded*

12 cherry tomatoes, *halved*

For the dressing

3 tbsp balsamic vinegar

3 tbsp white wine vinegar

2 tbsp extra virgin olive oil

120g Gorgonzola cheese, *roughly chopped*

½ red onion, *finely sliced*

4 tbsp roughly chopped fresh parsley

salt and freshly ground black pepper

rice crackers, to serve

Preheat the oven to 220°C/gas mark 7.

Place the potato halves in a medium pan of salted water, bring to the boil and cook until tender. Cook the broad beans according to the packet instructions. Drain the potatoes and beans.

Toss the cooked potatoes, broad beans, canned beans and olive oil together, then place in a baking tray, pop into the oven for 10 minutes or until warmed through.

Meanwhile place the lettuce and cherry tomatoes into a large bowl.

Next make the dressing. Combine the vinegars and oil in a large jug and whisk well. Season well with salt and pepper. Then add the cheese, onion and parsley and mix well.

Spoon the warmed mixture from the oven into the lettuce and tomatoes (this is why you need a large bowl!) and mix well and quickly. Pour the dressing over and again mix well, but carefully. The tomatoes and lettuce will start to wilt and the cheese will start to melt. Serve straight away.

This is an unusual summer dish that is very refreshing. The secret is to ensure that the avocados are very ripe (but not discoloured).

Avocado with Pine Nuts and Yogurt

PREPARATION TIME 10 MINUTES • SERVES 4–6

2 ripe avocados

2 small shallots, *finely chopped*

225g thick natural yogurt

2 tbsp chopped fresh mint

55g baby gherkins, *chopped*

85g pine nuts, *lightly toasted*

2 tbsp olive oil

salt and freshly ground black pepper

tortilla chips or crispbreads, to serve

Cut the avocados in half, remove the skin and cut the flesh into small pieces. Place in a bowl, add the shallot and gently mash together with a fork.

Stir in the yogurt, mint, gherkins and pine nuts. Finally, season well with salt and freshly ground black pepper and stir in the olive oil. Cover and chill well before serving within 2 hours.

Serve with plenty of tortilla chips or crispbreads for dipping and scooping!

Warm salads are great for when the weather's not quite behaving itself in the summer or for cooler spring and autumn days when a cold salad just wouldn't hit the spot. This one is a real cracker – enjoy!

Warm Aubergine Salad with Almond Pesto

SERVES 4 • PREPARATION TIME 25 MINUTES • COOKING TIME 20 MINUTES

12 small new potatoes, *skin on and halved*

200g green beans, *sliced diagonally in half*

1 large aubergine, *cut into 1cm dice*

4 tbsp olive oil

200g mozzarella cheese, *cut into 1cm dice*

50g mixed salad leaves

1 tsp finely chopped fresh red chilli

2 tbsp sultanas

12 cherry tomatoes, *halved*

salt and freshly ground black pepper

For the pesto

2 garlic cloves, *finely chopped*

20 leaves fresh basil

50g whole unskinned almonds, *lightly toasted*

6–8 tbsp olive oil

20g Pecorino cheese, *finely grated*

Preheat the oven to 220°C/gas mark 7.

Place the potato halves in a medium pan of salted water, bring to the boil and cook until tender. Place the beans in a separate pan of salted water, bring to the boil and cook until tender. Drain the potatoes and beans.

Toss the cooked potatoes, aubergine, olive oil and plenty of black pepper together in a roasting tin and cook for 15 minutes.

When the vegetables are nearly cooked, after 10–12 minutes, add the mozzarella cheese and warm it through for 2–3 minutes. Do not overcook it or the cheese will melt too much.

Place all the ingredients for the pesto into a food processor and blend until fairly smooth.

Tip the cheesy roasted vegetables into a bowl and stir well. Add the mixed leaves, stirring through just a couple of times.

Finally add the beans, chilli, sultanas and tomatoes and season well with salt and pepper. Mix together gently, and divide between four serving plates. Spoon over the pesto to serve.

Mozzarella pearls (little nuggets of mozzarella) add a creamy, fresh flavour to this light salad. It's nice served on its own, maybe with some crusty bread, or as an accompaniment to grilled fish or meats.

Mozzarella Pearls, Broad Bean, Mustard and Mint Salad

SERVES 4 • **PREPARATION TIME** 20 MINUTES

300g frozen baby broad beans

20 baby Mozzarella pearls

20 baby plum tomatoes, *halved*

1 head romaine lettuce, *finely sliced*

For the dressing

2 tbsp Dijon mustard

pinch of sugar

3 tbsp white wine vinegar

100ml extra virgin olive oil

100ml sunflower oil

2 tbsp finely chopped fresh mint

salt and freshly ground black pepper

crusty bread, to serve

Cook the broad beans according to the packet instructions. Drain and refresh under cold running water.

Divide the beans, mozzarella, tomatoes and lettuce between 4 serving plates.

Make the dressing: place the mustard and sugar in a small jug, season well and whisk. Add the vinegar and oils and stir until well mixed. Taste and adjust the seasoning, then add the fresh mint and mix well.

To serve, spoon the dressing over the salad and mix well but carefully. Serve with crusty bread.

This is full of crunchy textures and simple clean flavours – a great addition to any outdoor feast.

Crispy Mackerel Slaw Salad with Lime, Chilli and Cashew Nuts

SERVES 4 • PREPARATION TIME 20 MINUTES • COOKING TIME 3–4 MINUTES

vegetable oil, for shallow frying

2 smoked mackerel fillets, *skinned*

¼ firm white cabbage, *very finely sliced*

2 medium carrots, *very finely sliced*

2 medium shallots, *very finely sliced lengthways*

3 tbsp salted cashew nuts, *roughly chopped*

1 tsp finely chopped fresh red chilli

3 tbsp clear honey

1 tbsp *nam pla* (Thai fish sauce)

finely grated zest of 1 lime plus 2 tbsp lime juice

3 tbsp chopped fresh coriander

salt and freshly ground black pepper

Melon and Cucumber Lassi, to serve (see page 145), optional

Pour oil into a shallow frying pan to a depth of about 1–2cm and heat.

Break the fish into small flakes, then fry them in the oil until they are nice and crispy. Drain well and season with a little salt and pepper.

Place the cabbage, carrot, shallot and nuts into a large serving bowl and mix well.

In small jug, mix the chilli, honey, *nam pla*, lime zest and juice. Season with black pepper and mix well.

Pour the dressing over the cabbage and carrots and mix well. Taste and season with a little more pepper if you think it needs it.

Just before serving add the warm flaked fish and chopped coriander and mix well.

Serve with a cooling Melon and Cucumber Lassi to drink.

Barbecue Beans

SERVES 4–6 • PREPARATION TIME 5 MINUTES
• COOKING TIME 10 MINUTES

Really easy and extremely tasty, the flavour combination here is truly delicious. In fact you'll probably be amazed that something so simple could taste so good! These beans could possibly become one of your classic barbecue dishes and your friends will be talking about them for a long time...

2 x 400g cans baked beans in tomato sauce
½ tsp dried red chilli flakes
1 tbsp clear honey
50g unsalted butter
½ tsp ground cumin
1 tbsp vinegar (any type)
4 tbsp chopped fresh coriander

Place all the ingredients apart from the coriander into a small pan. Warm over a gentle heat, until all the butter has melted.

Stir in the coriander and serve.

Spicy Sausage, Onion and Potato Hash

SERVES 4–6 • PREPARATION TIME 25 MINUTES
• COOKING TIME 20 MINUTES

This makes a nice side dish for a barbecue and is good for using up any leftover, cooked potatoes. It's also quite nice on its own with a green salad.

Any type of sausage will do here – I particularly like to use Cumberlands or you could use strips of cooked chicken, pork or beef.

2 tbsp vegetable oil
4 sausages
1 large onion, *finely chopped*
2 garlic cloves, *finely chopped*
500g cooked baby new potatoes, *halved*
200ml chicken stock
4–6 tbsp roughly chopped fresh parsley
salt and freshly ground black pepper

Heat a large frying pan, and then add the oil.

Meanwhile remove the skins from the sausages and cut them into 1cm slices. Roll the sausage slices into small balls. Add the sausage balls to the pan and cook for 5–6 minutes or until cooked and lightly browned, then remove and place on a plate.

Add the onion and garlic to the pan and cook until they take a little colour, then add the potatoes and stock and bring to the boil. Simmer and slightly mash the potatoes with a fork, then return the sausage balls to the pan. Warm through, then season well and add the parsley.

The end result should be a nice moist hash.

Add a few choice flavours to mayo and you've got a wonderful accompaniment to dollop on grilled meats, fish and vegetables.

Bacon, Chilli and Coriander Mayonnaise

SERVES 4–6 • **PREPARATION TIME** 10 MINUTES • **COOKING TIME** 10–15 MINUTES

2 tbsp vegetable oil

4 rashers streaky bacon, *chopped into small pieces*

1 tsp finely chopped fresh red chilli

350–400g mayonnaise

4 tbsp freshly chopped coriander

squeeze of lemon juice

freshly ground black pepper

Heat a small frying pan and add the oil and bacon. Now, this is the important bit, cook the bacon gently until it is really crisp and cooked right through.

Once cooked, remove the bacon from the pan and set aside to cool. Add the chilli to the pan and cook for a couple of minutes to soften and then cool.

Place the mayonnaise in a serving bowl, add the cooled bacon and chilli and the oil and fat from the pan. Add the coriander, a squeeze of lemon juice and some black pepper (you probably won't need to season with salt as the bacon will be salty enough), mix really well.

Cover and chill until ready to serve.

Hush Puppies

SERVES 4–6 • PREPARATION TIME 15 MINUTES PLUS
STANDING • COOKING TIME 10 MINUTES

A great Southern American favourite, these are traditionally served with iced sweet tea and Southern fried or barbecued chicken.

The history of these small fritters has many theories. The one that sounds most plausible is that they were made by soldiers in the American Civil War, and the leftovers were given to their dogs, or puppies to 'hush' them.

140g finely ground cornmeal or polenta
140g self-raising flour
3 pinches of salt
1 tbsp sugar
1 tsp ground black pepper
1 medium egg, *beaten*
284ml carton buttermilk
2½ tbsp creamed horseradish
3 spring onions, *finely chopped*
vegetable oil, for deep frying
mayonnaise, to serve

Place the cornmeal, flour, salt, sugar and pepper in a medium mixing bowl and mix well. Add the egg, buttermilk and horseradish and stir well. Finally add the spring onions. Cover and leave to stand for 1 hour.

Heat the oil in a deep fat fryer to 170°C or fill a deep pan one-third full with oil and use a cooking thermometer to check the oil temperature.

Spoon small amounts of the mixture into the hot oil and cook until golden brown. Remove from the hot oil and drain on kitchen paper. Eat warm dipped in mayonnaise.

Tomato, Aubergine and Parmesan Pasta

SERVES 4 • PREPARATION TIME 15 MINUTES
• COOKING TIME 30 MINUTES

This sauce is based on the classic Italian dish 'Melanzane alla Parmigiana' where aubergines and tomatoes are layered, topped with Parmesan and baked. This version works really well as a simple sauce for pasta.

3 tbsp olive oil
1 onion, *finely chopped*
1 aubergine, *finely chopped*
2 garlic cloves, *finely chopped*
400g can chopped tomatoes with herbs
100ml white wine
1 vegetable stock cube
1 tbsp tomato purée
1 small bunch fresh basil, *roughly chopped*
1 tbsp vinegar (any type)
1 tbsp sugar
50g Parmesan cheese, *finely grated*
freshly ground black pepper
conchiglie or rigatoni pasta, extra Parmesan
    and fresh chopped basil, to serve

Heat the oil in a medium pan. Add the onion, aubergine and garlic, mix well and cook over a medium heat for 10 minutes. Next, add the tomatoes, wine and 100ml water, mix really well. Add the stock cube, purée, basil, vinegar and sugar, season with black pepper and mix really well. Bring to the boil, then turn down the heat to a simmer. Cook for 20 minutes or until the aubergines are very soft.

Stir the Parmesan through the sauce and serve with cooked pasta, sprinkled with extra cheese and basil.

All the rage in the southern states of the USA, I first had these in North Carolina some years ago. It's a nice way to use up any home-grown tomatoes at the end of the season, that just won't ripen.

This recipe was given to me by my great friend Richard Delany, who I worked with 20 years ago.

Fried Green Tomatoes

SERVES 4 • **PREPARATION TIME** 15 MINUTES • **COOKING TIME** 10 MINUTES

284ml carton buttermilk

150g finely ground cornmeal
  or polenta

150g self-raising flour

1 tsp dried oregano

6 medium-sized green tomatoes,
  cut lengthways into ½cm slices

6 tbsp olive oil

50g unsalted butter

½ tsp chilli powder

salt and freshly ground black pepper

Place the buttermilk in a small bowl.

Place the cornmeal, flour and oregano into another bowl. Season well.

Place the tomato slices in the flour mix, then in the milk, then back in the flour mix, coating really well.

Once all the slices are coated, heat the oil and butter in a shallow frying pan. Add 5–6 tomato slices and cook for 2–3 minutes on each side. Remove from the pan and sprinkle with salt and chilli powder.

Repeat to cook the remaining slices. Serve hot.

These are nice and simple to prepare – you can do most of the preparation in advance and then finish them off when your guests arrive.

I sometimes take a small deep fat fryer outside and have it next to my barbecue. Do take care though that it's not going to rain and that children and animals are kept well away from the fryer and electricity cables at all times.

Spicy Courgette Fries

SERVES 6–8 • PREPARATION TIME 15 MINUTES • COOKING TIME 20 MINUTES

vegetable oil, for deep frying
6 medium courgettes, *washed and dried really well*
400g self-raising flour
568ml carton milk
cayenne pepper
salt and freshly ground pepper

Heat the oil in a deep fat fryer to 175˚C or if cooking indoors fill a deep pan one-third full with oil and use a cooking thermometer to check the oil temperature.

Cut the courgettes into 1cm thick slices on the diagonal.

Place the flour in one bowl and the milk in another bowl. Season the milk with a little salt and pepper. Flour the courgette pieces well, a few at a time, and then dip into the milk, then straight back into the flour and coat well. Repeat until all the courgettes are coated twice, and then dust off well.

Cook the courgettes in small handfuls until just cooked and very lightly coloured –this is known as blanching or setting. Drain on kitchen paper.

When you are ready to eat, increase the temperature of the oil to 185–190˚C. Cook again, this time until the courgette pieces are crispy and golden brown. Drain on kitchen paper and season well with salt, pepper and cayenne pepper and serve immediately.

I first had cornbread in a diner in Chapel Hill, North Carolina for breakfast, and have been a fan ever since. I like to use olive oil rather than butter to get a slightly lighter end result.

Rosemary Buttermilk Cornbread Muffins

MAKES 12 • **PREPARATION TIME** 15 MINUTES • **COOKING TIME** 20 MINUTES

2 medium eggs

2 x 284ml cartons buttermilk

4 tbsp olive oil

70g self-raising flour

1 tsp sugar

1 tsp salt

200g finely ground cornmeal
   or polenta

4 sprigs fresh rosemary, *leaves
   roughly chopped*

2 garlic cloves, *finely crushed*

Preheat the oven to 200°C/gas mark 6. Line a 12-hole muffin tray with 12 paper muffin cases.

Place the eggs, buttermilk and oil into a bowl and whisk well.

Place the flour, sugar, salt, cornmeal, chopped rosemary and garlic into another bowl and mix well.

Pour the wet mixture into the dry mixture and mix well, but don't go mad. Spoon into the prepared cases and bake for 15–20 minutes, or until well risen.

Remove from the oven and cool slightly before eating.

These will keep for 2 days in an airtight container or freeze for up to 3 months.

Potato Salad with Hot Vinaigrette

SERVES 4–6 • PREPARATION TIME 10 MINUTES • COOKING TIME 20 MINUTES

Whether you scrape or scrub new potatoes is a personal choice but here's a tip about cooking them for salads. For the best flavour, cook the potatoes, drain well, then place them back into the cooking pan, cover with clingfilm and leave to cool to room temperature. This way of cooking and cooling really improves the quality and flavour in the end salad.

500g baby new or Jersey Royal potatoes, *scrubbed*
4 rashers streaky bacon, *chopped*
4 tbsp olive oil
2 tbsp cider vinegar
1 tbsp wholegrain mustard
salt and freshly ground black pepper

Place the potatoes in a medium pan of salted water, bring to the boil and cook until tender. Drain, return to the pan, cover with clingfilm and leave to cool to room temperature.

Meanwhile, place a non-stick frying pan over a low heat. Add the bacon and the olive oil to the pan and cook the bacon for 10–15 minutes or until it starts to crisp up.

Once the bacon is cooked and crispy, remove it from the pan, then add the onion and cook it for 1 minute in the remaining bacon fat and oil. Add the vinegar and mustard to the pan with a little salt and pepper, swirl together.

Cut the potatoes in half and place them in a serving bowl. Pour over the hot dressing and add the bacon, stir well and serve warm.

Roasted Baby New Potatoes with Pecorino and Rocket

SERVES 4 • PREPARATION TIME 15 MINUTES • COOKING TIME 50 MINUTES

These are delicious served indoors or outdoors – but for some reason they always seem to taste best when the barbecue is lit!

500g baby new potatoes
2 tbsp olive oil
55g unsalted butter
2 sprigs fresh rosemary
1 bulb garlic, *halved horizontally*
50g rocket
75g Pecorino cheese
salt and freshly ground black pepper

Preheat the oven to 200°C/gas mark 6.

Wash the potatoes really well and remove any loose skin.

Heat a small baking tray on the hob, then add the oil, butter, rosemary and garlic and heat until they bubble away nicely.

Add the new potatoes and seasoning and stir well. Cover well with foil and place in the oven. Cook for 35–45 minutes, or until nicely cooked and soft. Stir really well.

Fold through the rocket so it wilts slightly. Using a potato peeler, peel the Pecorino into longs strips and carefully stir it through, leaving a few strips on the top. Serve and enjoy!

RESOURCES

UK

Barbecues and Smokers

BQZEEN Ltd
Ash Tree Farm
North Green
Pulham St Mary
Diss, Norfolk IP21 4XX
www.bqzeen.com
sales@bqzeen.com
Tel: 01379 676 252

Bradley Smokers
www.bradleysmoker.co.uk
• Gives details of stockists by region

Cookequip Ltd
Unit 4, Sumner Place, Addlestone
Surrey KT15 1QD
Tel: 01932 841 171
sales@cookequip.co.uk
www.cookequip.co.uk
• Smokers, barbecues, wood chips

Flaming Barbecues
Kybotech Ltd, Parry Business Park
Grassthorpe Road
Sutton On Trent
Nottinghamshire NG23 6QX
Tel: 0800 169 6016
sales@kybotech.co.uk
www.flamingbarbecues.co.uk
• Gas barbecues, charcoal barbecues, kettle
  barbecues, portable barbecues
• Order online or by phone
• Free delivery to most parts of the UK

Planet Barbecue
www.planetbarbecue.co.uk
Tel: 01271 378 887/01271 891 167
• Smokers, charcoal barbecues, gas
  barbecues, woodchips, rotisseries, digital
  thermometers
• Free delivery within the UK for orders
  over £300
• International deliveries to EEC countries

Rotigrill
www.rotigrill.com
Tel: 0844 800 8411
• Rotisseries, hog roasts, kebab skewers
• Order online
• Free delivery to UK mainland addresses

Weber Barbecues
Weber-Stephen North West Europe
The Four Columns
Broughton Hall Business Park
Skipton BD23 3AE
Tel: 01756 692 600
salesuk@weberstephen.com
www.weberbbq.co.uk

Weber Grill Academy
Weber House
Baldon Lane
Marsh Baldon
Oxford OX44 9LT
Tel: 01865 341 341
grillacademy@weberstephen.com
www.grillacademy.co.uk

Barbecue Bags

Qbag
Victoria House
19–21 Ack Lane East
Bramhall, Stockport, England SK7 2BE
Tel: 0161 440 7302
web@qbag.com
www.qbag.com
• Available in packs of five cooking bags
• Order online
• International distributors in Australia,
  New Zealand, France, South Africa,
  Scandinavia

Barbecue Skewers

BBQ.co.uk
Tel: 02380 788 155
charles@bbq.co.uk
www.bbq.co.uk
• Bamboo skewers, double-prong skewers
• UK delivery
• For international deliveries, contact
  charles@socal.co.uk

Chimney Starters

BBQ World
Dawson's Department Store
Queens Hall, 56 King St
Clitheroe, Lancashire BB7 2EU
www.bbqworld.co.uk
Tel: 0844 736 6126
• Order online or shop in store
• UK and EU deliveries

Dutch Ovens

Dutch Ovens UK
4 Canalside, Northbridge Road
Berkhamsted, Hertfordshire HP4 1EG
Tel: 01442 872 829
www.dutchovens.co.uk
• Dutch ovens, fish smokers, skillets and
  griddles, dutch campfire sandwich
  toasters and campfire forks
• Order online or shop in store
• Deliveries within the UK only

**Ronnie Sunshines Great
Outdoor Store**
4 Canalside, Northbridge Road
Berkhamsted, Hertfordshire HP4 1EG
Tel: 01442 872829
www.ronniesunshines.com
• Dutch ovens, fish smokers, skillets and
  griddles, campfire sandwich toasters,
  ghillie kettles, stainless steel billy tins
• Order online
• International deliveries, except to
  Australia and the Far East

Giant Cupcake Tins

Cakes, Cookies & Crafts Shop
Unit 5, Woodgate Park
White Lund Ind Estate
Morecambe, Lancashire LA3 3PS
Tel: 01524 389684
www.cakescookiesandcraftsshop.co.uk
• Order online
• UK and international deliveries

Lakeland
Alexandra Buildings
Windermere
Cumbria LA23 1BQ
Tel: 01539 488 100
• Over 40 stores nationwide
• Order online
• UK and international deliveries only
  available to those using payment cards
  issued by UK banks

Squires Kitchen
Squires House
3 Waverley Lane
Farnham, Surrey GU98BB
Tel: 0845 61 71 810
Tel: 01252 260 260 (overseas)
www.squires-shop.com
• Order online or shop in store
• UK and international deliveries

Hog Roast Specialists

Hog Roast Hire Company
Chipping Norton, Oxfordshire
www.hogroast-hire.co.uk
Tel: 01608 642 647/ 07802 766 994
enquiries@hogroast-hire.co.uk
• Several packages available including
  machine hire, and machine hire plus
  set-up plus chef
• Prices quoted on website are for a radius
  of 20 miles from Chipping Norton,
  Oxfordshire. Any extra mileage will incur
  an additional charge

Mere Brow Smithy
29 The Gravel
Mere Brow
Preston, Lancashire PR4 6JX
Tel: 01772 812 031/ 07791 801 958
sales@merebrowsmithy.com
www.merebrowsmithy.com
• Hog Roast Hire
• A full demo and instructions are provided
  when equipment is hired
• Roast machines to be collected from and
  returned to Mere Brow Smithy

The Spitting Pig Co.
Tel: 0800 587 5899
sales@spittingpig.co.uk
www.spittingpig.co.uk
• Buy or hire a hog roast
• Free delivery within the UK and EU
• International delivery from £250 + VAT

USA

Chuckwagon Supplies
3775 W 4000 S
West Haven, Utah 84401
USA
Tel: +1 801 920 9004
service@chuckwagonsupply.com
www.chuckwagonsupply.com
• Dutch ovens, griddles, meat forks, heat-
  resistant spatulas
• Order online

Grill Time LLC
www.superskewer.com
• Flat skewers, square skewers, twin
  skewers
• Free shipping within the US
• International orders available with the
  first US$12 of the shipping tariff covered
  by Grill Time.

A Happy Camper
1848 Addison Avenue East
Twin Falls, Idaho 83301
USA
Tel: +1 208 736 8048
www.ahappycamper.com
• Dutch ovens and accessories, mobile
  stoves, campfire grills, griddles
• Order online or shop in store

The Home Depot
Tel: +1 1800 466 3337
www.homedepot.com
• Charcoal barbecues, gas barbecues,
  smokers
• Visit website for store locator

CANADA

Barbecues Galore
3505 Edmonton Trail NE
Calgary, Alberta T2E 3N9
Tel: +1 403 250 1558
calgarynorth@barbecuesgalore.ca
www.barbecuesgalore.ca
• Charcoal barbecues, smokers, rotisseries
• Visit website for store locator

The Home Depot
Tel +1 1800 668 2266 (store customer
enquiries)
Tel +1 1800 628 0525 (online customer
enquiries)
www.homedepot.ca
• Gas barbecues, charcoal barbecues,
  portable barbecues, barbecue accessories
• Visit website for store locator

AUSTRALIA

Bunnings
www.bunnings.com.au
+61 1800 500 885
• Kettle and portable barbecues
• Visit website for store finder

The Redback Trading Company
PO Box 613
Healesville
Victoria
Australia 3777
Tel: +61 417 144 698
info@redbacktrading.com.au
http://redbacktrading.com.au/
• Dutch ovens, smokers
• Order online

INDEX

ACKNOWLEGEMENTS

There are so many people I would like to thank. This sort of book takes many hours and years of work and thought, so without help there is no way I could have completed it.

Firstly Kyle again for having great faith, especially when I said I needed a few more months. Jenny Wheatley for tying up all the loose ends and making the whole thing work, even organising a photoshoot in Tenerife at the last moment. Kate Barraclough for making the layout look fantastic.

Many thanks once again to Jane Bamforth, for fitting in the time and making sense of my scribbling and bad grammar.

Steve, Doug and Wendy Lee – brilliant shots and prepping over the past few years. Bea Harling, good friend and brilliant as always, Clare Greenstreet for cooking, shopping and finding all the ingredients I couldn't. John Rush, my close friend and agent, and Luigi Bonomi for getting this off the ground.

Thanks to all the suppliers of ingredients and equipment for your help, some way beyond the call of duty.

Everyone has a best friend, in my case that also happens to be my gorgeous wife Fern who never fails to look after and encourage me. I'm a lucky bloke.

My thanks to you all.

Phil Vickery